Synecdoche,
New York

TIMECODES

A book series exploring individual movies minute by minute.

Also in the Series:
Gerry, by Nicholas Rombes
BlacKkKlansman, by Alex Zamalin
Twin Peaks: The Return, Part 8, by Jeff Wood
Neptune Frost, by Steven Shaviro

Synecdoche, New York

Movies Minute by Minute

Grant Maierhofer

BLOOMSBURY ACADEMIC
NEW YORK • LONDON • OXFORD • NEW DELHI • SYDNEY

BLOOMSBURY ACADEMIC

Bloomsbury Publishing Inc, 1359 Broadway, New York, NY 10018, USA
Bloomsbury Publishing Plc, 50 Bedford Square, London, WC1B 3DP, UK
Bloomsbury Publishing Ireland, 29 Earlsfort Terrace, Dublin 2, D02 AY28, Ireland

BLOOMSBURY, BLOOMSBURY ACADEMIC and the Diana logo are
trademarks of Bloomsbury Publishing Plc

First published in the United States of America 2026

Cover design by Eleanor Rose
Cover illustration © Freya Betts

Bloomsbury Publishing Inc does not have any control over, or responsibility
for, any third-party websites referred to or in this book. All internet
addresses given in this book were correct at the time of going to press. The
author and publisher regret any inconvenience caused if addresses have
changed or sites have ceased to exist, but can accept no responsibility for
any such changes.

A catalog record for this book is available from the Library of Congress.

ISBN: HB: 979-8-7651-8845-3
PB: 979-8-7651-8866-8
ePDF: 979-8-7651-8869-9
eBook: 979-8-7651-8871-2

Series: Timecodes

Typeset by Deanta Global Publishing Services, Chennai, India
Printed and bound in the United States of America

For product safety related questions contact productsafety@bloomsbury.com.

To find out more about our authors and books visit www.bloomsbury.com
and sign up for our newsletters.

For Kelsey, Ada, Hollis and Elisabeth

and with thanks and love to
the work of Charlie Kaufman

CONTENTS

PREFACE

Synecdoche, New York will always stand out as a rare example of a genius screenwriter's first foray into directing. While the list of genius screenwriters who made this pivot is brief—among them David Mamet, Joseph L. Mankiewicz, and Federico Fellini—the bringing together of the idiosyncrasies and characteristics that so distinguished Charlie Kaufman's writing from the field into his work as a director stands apart, especially among the Americans. It blends scathing hilarity, abysmal tragedy, and a determination to remain devoted to art as one of, if not the highest, human callings. It also features Philip Seymour Hoffman at the very peak of his powers, and thus when the editor of this series, Nicholas Rombes—of two, the other being Nadine Boljkovac—very first approached me about writing for his "Minute 9" series for *3AM Magazine*, I almost instantly knew I'd be writing about Kaufman's film. When I got in touch later, maybe a year or so after the piece had gone up, and found out he'd developed his interest in constrained criticism into the Timecodes series with Boljkovac, I put together a proposal to expand my essay about as quickly and excitedly as I'd written my "Minute 9."

I have, at any given moment, three or four films I'd probably comfortably cite as favorites, but only with *Synecdoche, New York* did the prospect of analyzing it minute-by-minute seem to make perfect sense. I'd certainly never call it an "easy" film, and it wouldn't be my first recommendation if someone found themselves curious about Kaufman's output—for both of these, the relative ease and the accessibility for just about anybody, I'd go with *Adaptation*, which also functions as an introduction to a version of the man himself. What seemed to make it perfect for this mode of analysis is precisely how I'd characterize my love for it. Some films, to me anyway, function like memories. The more we attempt to prod at them, the more elusive they can sometimes feel. Or perhaps dreams are closer, though if I'm honest I've never felt all that compelled to remember dreams. I have an obsessive nature that sometimes spirals into a disorder, and there are moments when fixating on memories, both good and bad, will consume me. Often the way out is to write about them. In a way, although some of these memories are often dark, misremembered things my brain is using to attack my comfort, the impulse of remembering accurately seems to be based in a kind of love, or a desire to have more understanding of myself. Halfway through first watching Wim Wenders' *Paris, Texas*, for example, I said aloud, "this is my favorite film." A day or a week later, aside from the colors, I'd have been hard-pressed to tell someone anything much of note that happened in it. Like a memory we want to cling to, or like a dream, or perhaps even someone we've met that we fall quickly for, the more we grasp at it, the more elusive it seems to get. The more I thought, in the abstract, about *Synecdoche, New York*, having gone through a similar "this is my favorite film" while watching it, the less sure I felt about what I'd seen. I only knew what it had made me feel and how I'd loved it, and had a vague sense of its varicolored moods across its runtime.

Other favorites, for whatever reason, don't tend to feel that way. It is a film embodying a spirit in American art-making that traces back to Emerson and probably beyond. Now that I've done it—and there were days, plenty of them, where I wondered if I'd manage to write this book—although I might possess a slightly firmer understanding of its workings, I'm happy to report that its magic, that stuff I so often feel prompted to grab at, still probably eludes about 40 percent of my consciousness. What's changed, however, is I now have this closeness—a friend, a kind of locket—of my experience of engaging with the film so consistently and directly. I feel, I'd imagine, how John Cage must've felt when he'd solved the puzzle of reading *Finnegans Wake* by composing his own texts, the first volume of *Writing Through Finnegans Wake*. I feel I've moved through the labyrinth of Kaufman's film and now carry some of that, and the experience of it, with me forever, and thus I feel extraordinarily lucky. You'll notice, I'm sure, that not unlike *Finnegans Wake* there is an endless sprawl of theories around various meanings in *Synecdoche, New York*. As with Joyce, the best of these are driven by people who simply love the film, and have engaged with it so intimately, and seriously, that they can't help but extend their thinking to this place. I've acknowledged these, where possible, but my impulse has been to remain true to my preferences in reading about or considering films. First and foremost, I wanted to let the film wash over me, to bask in it and to observe, because for me that's the purest way of appreciating anything.

I hope that you enjoy this as much as I enjoyed writing it, and that tonight you'll put on a double feature of *Synecdoche, New York* and *Adaptation*.

Grant Maierhofer, 2025

Minutes 1–119

Minute 1

Before we see an image created for the purposes of *Synecdoche, New York*, we see the company who in part funded the film and hear the voice of a child, presumably this is Olive, the first daughter character, singing a sweet song about Schenectady, New York:

> *There's a place I long to be,*
> *A certain town that's dear to me,*
> *Home to Mohawks and GE,*
> *It's called Schenectady,*
> *I was born there and I'll die there,*
> *My first home I hope to buy there,*
> *Have a kid or at least try there,*
> *Sweet Schenectady,*
> *And when I'm buried and I'm dead,*
> *Upstate worms will eat my head . . .*[1]

This is as good a place as any to present one of my thoughts about how to situate *Synecdoche, New York* as a film. I think it's possible to view it as the inverse of *Eraserhead*, for two main reasons: (1) the use of sound to communicate something at least slightly incommensurate with whatever's on screen that might be said to be the "true" feeling of the film's voice, and (2) the idea that it's a film about, and in response to, the anxiety of becoming a parent when one is quite convicted in one's determination to be an artist, which is seen—at least societally—as potentially at odds with one's ability to make art. This is, as you'll see, a thought that a film like *Synecdoche, New York*—hereinafter referred to as *S.N.Y.*—seems to prompt, being an elusive work by someone contemporaneously and since hailed as a genius. One reaches for associations, a bit like one reaches for a blanket in which to hide. As thoughts go, however, the *Eraserhead* one isn't awful, and certainly the two films would make for an excellent, if troubling, double feature.

Olive, the first daughter character, who's Caden Cotard's daughter, the director and playwright who might be said to be the protagonist, is one of the three members of the family that might be said to be the *heart* of *S.N.Y.* Her innocence, which is certainly conveyed by having her charmingly work her way through this sweet song to start the film, is a necessary element to the functionality of family—and probably any family—as an essential aspect to this film. It's also, considering where the film goes—and throughout comedy will function similarly—nicely disarming. We've heard about this film, probably, before seeing it. We've heard about its creator, his *difficulty*, but all that we hear is the sweet singing voice of a little kid. How "difficult" could it be?

The first image we see in the first minute is an Emerson alarm clock, and it's 7:44 in the morning, and in a few seconds it's 7:45, and a radio announcer is switched on, who's interviewing a literature professor about the season. It is fall. We pull back and we see a sleeping man, gesturing with his mouth, not frowning exactly but gesturing downward, and next to him there's a nightstand full of books, and already things feel rather cluttered or busy.

The radio announcer's question at the very end of the first minute: *Why do so many people write about the fall?* There is, of course, the seasonal fall, i.e., autumn, which is literally being referred to, and there is the Fall of man, in the biblical context, or simply the fall outside the Bible, of any man, though arguably regardless of one's leaning, the literal thing being referenced in some sense refers to any of these. The harvest, before the long dark months of winter, the literal and metaphorical readying for death.

Minute 2

Our professor-on-the-radio is prompted to read something, and reads:

Whoever has no house now, will never have one. Whoever is alone will stay alone,
will sit, read, write long letters through the evening,
and wander the boulevards, up and down,
restlessly, while the dry leaves are blowing.[2]

During this reading Philip Seymour Hoffman's character, Caden Cotard, the father, has sat up in bed and looks quizzically at himself on the edge of his bed in a slim mirror hung up on a door in his bedroom. We aren't told that this is a poem by Rainer Maria Rilke, and in the interest of total candor—this is Kaufman after all—I wouldn't have known the poem without looking it up. I never know what to make of a situation like that. Most often, I might feel angry that the writer/director/artist hasn't told me who wrote or made the thing being shared/referenced. In this instance, though, I think it's woven seamlessly into the content of the film well enough and fits the scene. *S.N.Y.* is an extremely recursive film that sort of encircles or enfolds itself in varied ways—later, a character outright states "The end is built into the beginning"—and it's quite incredible how perfectly these lines from Rilke overlay the final moments of the film.

Caden rises from bed, and there's a cut to a wooden staircase, and it looks as though we're in the home of an academic, or an artist, or multiple of either, or both. There's an implication of mess, though the mess seems thought about, at least, and warm. We see Catherine Keener's Adele, the mother, coughing into her sleeve. Her hair is crazed, as Keener's tends to be, but again there's this warmth to her, though this situation we're waking up into feels strained—it could go either way, be either thing. She says she didn't want to wake him, and Caden says that she didn't, and the usual husband/wife greetings are made. Adele ducks into the bathroom and at the end of this minute is sitting on the edge of the shower as their daughter finishes using the toilet. It's hitting me how perfectly the past two minutes have captured the physicality of home life, as I sit on the edge of my bed almost every day looking into a slim mirror quizzically, and must've sat on the edge of our shower thousands of times helping the kids figure out the bathroom

Minute 3

Their lives are the hectic lives of any family with young children. Their daughter finishes using the toilet, and Adele wipes her and finds her poop is green, which gives her pause, which gives Olive pause, and the phone is ringing. She's asked Caden to get it, and initially, he doesn't want to. He's in his head, but agrees and hands the phone off to Adele when she's left the bathroom and everything's squared away. There's very little in this that could be considered "cinematic," which works in its favor. It's a depiction of an extreme state of domestic life, the kind of circumstance you'd feel worried at, should family, or friends, or your neighbors knock on the door. Every shot is busy and layered like the clothing of a Midwestern professor in fall, different textures disinterested in being the focus of our attention, and Hoffman's Caden looks, as opposed to sickly, overfull of this existence, not obscenely so, but as if the anxieties of his living have been ingested. Keener's Adele is perfectly cluttersome. She picks up the phone and quickly flits into peals of laughter and welcome as Caden goes to check the mail.

We don't know who it is, but someone is standing by a telephone pole observing Caden do this. Tom Noonan is staring on, wearing the dark gray version of a pervert's trench coat, as Caden descends the steps into the sun in only a white T-shirt, boxers, footwear, as he puts on a black jacket against what cold there might be. He opens the mail and we see the face of an old man wearing an oxygen mask on the cover of a magazine called *Attending to Your Illness*, which he picks up and stares at momentarily, grabbing the rest and heading inside.

He opens the paper, *The Schenectedian*, which reads Friday, October 14, 2005, with a headline below stating *Harold Pinter at 76, a Sense of Validation*, and states: "Harold Pinter died."

Adele: "Wow. Well, he's old right?"
Caden: "No, wait. He won the Nobel Prize."

What's interesting is this seems to correspond to a real article once published in the Arts & Leisure section of the *New York Times*, called "For Harold Pinter at 76, a sense of valediction," from 2006, in the aftermath of Pinter's winning the Nobel Prize in 2005. It's worth delving into at least because of the seriousness with which this film, and its protagonist, will take theater as a human endeavor, but also because, for all of his engagement with slightly surreal or absurd subject matter, especially *Synecdoche*, Kaufman has always struck me as a filmmaker *most* invested in the artist-function of any of his pursuits, engaging with experience, and here engaging with history and real figures, to offer us something beyond mere

shallow reference. Caden's misunderstandings, too, the quick
jump from death to the Nobel Prize—which also puts one in
mind of the origins of the Prize itself—seem essential to who
he is. At times they seem to terrify him, or infuriate him, but
mostly they're the humdrum elements of his existence, his
constant attempts at reckoning with his experience, which
in turn connects back to his sense of what theater—and by
extension what the artist (i.e., the artist-function)—can offer
its practitioners and its audiences.

Minute 4

The parents' concern over Olive's stool has affected the kid,
who's now concerned, but Caden is pretty aloof, drifting through
the paper as dads were once reliably doing, remembering
previous plays he'd put on, turning on the TV to a strange
cartoon on viruses while the mother serves Olive her oatmeal.
Everything is relatively stable because our protagonist seems
to want to insist on a state of stability. Even his concerns, his
feeling of ill-health, his preoccupation with particular images,
these things feel rote, not really the stuff of major worry so
much as more of the fabric he's put upon his life. The walls of
the house are damaged, but look almost like outlines of elderly
figures. The TV is old, but the image of the strange cartoon is
sharp. The milk is expired, but given the references to the date,
it might actually be a year old, or I'm missing something, or
the slippages of comprehension of the character, or me, are
simply persisting. There is a felt absence in the house because
of this, where they're each engaging with, at best, a version
of the person who isn't in front of them, or more likely, and
worst, indifferent to who's in front of them and engaging in
a narrative beside their lives—this is mainly with mom and
dad, however, as both have their daily engagements with Olive
pretty handled, while Olive herself is off and running in her

personality, rattling off questions about her green poop before answers could possibly be given back.

Minute 5

Next we have a sequence of clearer jumps in time that give us a better sense of what the film is doing, which disconcert— "Happy Halloween, Schenectady," the radio announcer says; and shortly after says it's November 1, while Caden reads that it's November 2 in the newspaper—but this is short-lived, as we cut then to Caden standing in the bathroom, wallpapered in green weeds, prepping himself to shave, when the sink begins malfunctioning, spurting water up at random, when suddenly a piece shoots off and hits Caden right in the forehead, drawing ample blood, and the water sprays more violently into the room as he screams "God! Somebody! Adele help!" She comes in angrily, as happens more often than not in these domestic situations, plucked as she is from her previous involvement, but noticing the blood, which is ample, shifts quickly to concern and tries to shut the water off. The quick ratcheting up of the days prior to this builds like these domestic situations, rampant and violent and out of our control until something regrettable takes place. The sensation, too, with date-to-date-to-date, feels almost as if we're literally living these multiple different mornings, cuts between them, or in concurrence, and really we might as well be, in terms of our relationship to any narrative film beginning in such a way—I don't mean he's *commenting* on this tendency, which seems banal, but more like it's a montaging without need, which quickly gives us the sense of our days amassing in spite of our efforts, yet another facet of Caden's (our) lack of control over this existence.

"Mommy, Daddy has blood."
"Yeah."

Minute 6

Caden sees a doctor, getting his wound on his forehead stitched up, where there is continuing misunderstanding between them. Further, in the first ten minutes of this film, the Father and the Daughter are both shown to have changes in their bowel movements, the Daughter's more green than usual, the Father's more yellow. Caden is asked this after something in his eye is noticed, improper pupil dilation, and he misunderstands the doctor, who says "ophthalmologist," to be saying "neurologist," and shortly thereafter we're in the car, concerned and unwounded Mother Adele driving, asking questions about the appointment, and Daughter Olive leaning in from the backseat, asking questions about what they're saying.

First she repeats a small song about it being Tuesday, and asks her Mother if it's Tuesday, to which Adele responds "No, honey, today is Friday." Again these weird slippages of time, and over some kind of narration, in the car, the melody of "Auld Lang Syne" is playing.

Minute 7

Caden's anxious, and unsure, and Adele is frustrated by all of it and certain that Caden misunderstood something, like aggressively certain, and this in comparison with Caden, who repeats, "He doesn't know, but, maybe?" several times, only adding to the frustration and the sense that something is wrong, but their clarity on the matter is nil. "It's the start of something awful," Caden says, before cursing and apologizing and cursing again, and complaining that he has rehearsal, and that it's "fucked timing." Again, the importance of the work he does is apparent, but what's different in this depiction is it's shown as something woven into the stress and beauty and simplicity of his family and his domestic life. It's woven into

Caden quite literally, as he's never exactly shown in *S.N.Y.* as a "genius," at least in cinematic terms. He's shown more like a worker, someone frustrated, who has responsibilities but is devoted to something which may bring him satisfaction but which inevitably leads to a kind of misunderstanding between the seriousness with which he approaches it and the reception of the world.

Minute 8

Caden is struggling to adequately describe plumbing, and plumbers, and what they do, to Olive, sitting in the backseat, and this veers into a weird correlation to her body, and her capillaries, and her blood, which devolves into her quietly freaking out and repeating "I don't want blood!" to which Adele responds, logically enough, that she doesn't have blood, to which Caden responds, logically enough, that he doesn't "think [she] should tell her that she doesn't have blood." Aside from certain moments in *Funny Games*, which is really the only example that leaps to mind, it's difficult to think of depictions of the kind of weird, private languages families can, of necessity, fall into, but Kaufman manages to turn it into something not universal, while still somehow nicely primitive, or "mystical" is the word that's coming to mind, like the language that might be used in a cautionary folktale.

Minute 9

Caden is seeing the ophthalmologist, who finishes using an apparatus to view his eyes, pulls away, and he asks if it was the "bump to the head," to which the doctor says he doesn't think so. What's interesting is the figures who might, in other films, provide comfort or surety, like doctors, like directors even, are sort of agents of disruption in Kaufman's work, where the anxious figure at the center of the film wants answers, and the answers can't possibly be sufficiently responsive to his/her *feeling* and thus their interactions are stilted, disrupted by an impossible gap between what one wants, or is required to offer as a part of their job, and what Caden, the patient, wants and feels is necessary to be OK. Again a misunderstanding, "neurologist" for "urologist," and the statement too that "the eyes are a part of the brain, after all," to which Caden says "well that's not true, is it?"

The ophthalmologist responds "Why would I say it if it weren't true?"

Caden's response: "It just doesn't . . . seem right."
Ophthalmologist: "Like morally correct, or 'right' as in accurate?"

I was recently able to watch *S.N.Y* in a theater, and I'd completely forgotten how much the film makes me laugh, and the communal experience of laughing about these little things, amid this creeping reality of fear and trembling, felt so wonderful. Doctors, therapists, authority figures frequently provide relief in Kaufman, then, through alternate means. It seems as if this probably comes from Kaufman's origins in sketch comedy, writing for *The Dana Carvey Show* in the nineties, but it also seems like a key to what sometimes makes people so uncomfortable watching his films. We have the sense, on the one hand, that his characters are terribly smart, and intellectual, and "difficult," and thus are not worth our time, as we're all now hyperaware of the minutes within our day. On the other hand, we have the sense that they are terribly sad, and existential, and painful both for their characters and for their audiences. Kaufman, too, seems both pained and intellectual, anxious and brilliant. What's easy to forget in this concoction, though, are the constant appeals to gut-level laughter, the constant attempts at making jokes that let one fully immerse in and transcend this pained experience. Like horror elements in a film like

Antichrist, or criminal elements in Tarantino, humor in Kaufman functions like humor in life, after a long, terrible day working at a miserable job with only more stress to return to and appointments to attend, an absurd, dark, disturbing joke can offer us salvation.

I'm still affected by the death of Philip Seymour Hoffman. I didn't know him, and I don't think I've even seen all of his work, but his presence is so affecting to me. He doesn't look like an actor. He struggled with addiction. He got sober young and relapsed. It scares me.

In *S.N.Y.*, we probably have his best work, playing a director putting on productions that grow from *Death of a Salesman* to an impossibly large thing, but in the ninth minute of the film we just have him talking to his doctor. The doctor asks if he means right as in morally correct or as in accurate. Hoffman's Caden Cotard says he doesn't know, maybe accurate, and then we're with these two for a moment, this awkward moment between someone who is hyper aware of themselves and his doctor, and although there's always that temptation to simply state anything to keep an appointment moving along, that doesn't happen, and suddenly both men are forced to sit and think, and it's uncomfortable but warm.

And then we have Cotard watching his production of *Death of a Salesman* in dress rehearsal, and Willie Loman is delivering his speech to his son who walks off in the middle of the scene about football. He realizes his son has gone and goes to his car; the car crashes into the house, and in the production, a piece of architecture hits Michelle Williams' character, so Cotard goes to check on her. It's clear there's a budding romance between them.

In the midst of this Cotard says it's too late in the game to be having these problems. At around nine minutes into the film it feels fine to link that with the movie itself. Or it's Cotard's life, and it's the place wherein he can express his frustration over the ongoing problems that are consuming him—his family, his health, his work, his identity—and his frustration is the same as Willie's, then, the father trying to wax poetically about the importance of the big game, and these big moments, who lashes out by crashing his car, as Cotard lashes out at the crash itself and everything breaking down around him.

Two protagonists, then, a mumbling Everyman who is subjected to the average medical appointment wherein he gives up everything to find out what's happening, only to be stopped with a quandary about the differences between moral rightness and simply being correct; and a theater director late in preparations for a play about the lateness of living and the world moving on whether or not we'd like it to, lashing out but then laughing and embracing the small comforts of a tryst with the starring actress.

It's interesting because there are scenes in this film I find physically painful to watch. There's a moment when Hoffman's character is putting together this massive production in a warehouse the size of the city, and it becomes so introspective that I can hardly bear to look at it. I think I chose *S.N.Y.* for a work of criticism like this because I knew it wouldn't mean I'd have to watch the entire film again, and I don't know what that says about me or about the work, to be simultaneously drawn toward something and its creator but not to be so drawn toward it that I want to simply watch it over and over again and can even comfortably do so.

I watch *S.N.Y.* every year or every couple of years or so. I get caught up in different elements, most recently Olive's tattoos—I liked the idea of trying to replicate them on myself as a way of forever connecting with the film. I don't even know if it's something I'd say I like in a typical application of that term. There are artworks that I like, and artworks that I even love, and then there are those perhaps I need, or have needed, and this film would fit in there, where its aesthetic rendering of certain preoccupations of the creator align perfectly with my own thinking.

We get the whiffs of the rest of the film here, in minute 9, the sense of frustration the outside world can often impose on people driven by aesthetics, and the awkward lives such people lead whenever they're not in their various temples. The sense of bliss that's double-edged when Cotard is in his temple and everything's not entirely perfect, and the predilection people in these situations have for simply telling jokes or laughing, because to name anything else too exactly might hinder the experience of everyone involved. The presence of the director, too, in Cotard but also in Kaufman: imposings upon imposings upon imposings. In his review of *Antichrist*, Roger Ebert made the point that even fictional films are a sort of documentary about the actors performing in these films, which I think also nicely expresses the layerings of influence and performance in *S.N.Y.*

In the realm of the practical, then, that is, the doctor's office, this artist is useless; he's mumbling and unsure and evasive. The doctor, comparatively, is comfortable and incisive, commenting on Cotard's observation and moving around it without much in the way of anxiety or reservation. In the theater, though, Cotard isn't bashful or unsure, and responds quickly to a potential injury with the same speed we'd hope a doctor might exercise in a similar situation. The film itself seems to also be about the growth of an aesthetic life to the extent it almost becomes unwieldy, where people viewing the warehouse much later in *S.N.Y.* couldn't help but ask why, and wonder at the role this kind of production might play in living. What's interesting is that this doesn't happen. Everybody there is committed, even if they're asking their director why, and he can't offer much in response. Living beats Cotard down, as does the work, but here, there's still a fire and a determination to see this production through, to make it unique and to make it expressive and powerful. The wavering in the doctor's office gives way to certitude and drive.

Something I struggle with with film in particular is the desire to take it in in any order I'd like. I hear about readers who read the end of a book first, and I've read some things piecemeal and never entirely through, and the distinctions with film seem arbitrary enough or at least made so by television and our screens, where films are broken into pieces anyway. Oddly, too, it seems natural, so when I rewatch this ninth minute consciously I feel as though I'm engaging in a criticism most in line with my natural aesthetic position, the one where I'm no longer carving out large swathes of time to watch one film from beginning to end, or reading much work that seems to demand a kind of attention that now feels unnatural, for better or worse.

Most of us don't like to visit the doctor, and I think it has to do with the forfeiture of authority. In this situation, the doctor has indicated that the eyes are part of the brain, and Hoffman's character suggests that this just doesn't seem right. It doesn't seem entirely right, and it's left there, with the moral question pursued and the usage question, rather than resolving it, and this leads to the dress rehearsal and the shift where Cotard is now the authority, and in his position of authority he behaves not unlike a doctor in an emergency. A flirtatious doctor, and a theater director who's able to treat his work with utmost seriousness, which again preoccupies me.

I don't know why, but I find myself thinking most of these days about the question of art and what it's for. Emil Cioran wrote about there being something wonderful in the pursuit of doing something that's entirely useless. To pursue something that is useless as opposed to doing any of the countless other things a person might do could have a kind of honor to it. And the world wants to tell us which things are useful and which things are useless. But the longer I live—and certainly this is a film to be lived with—the more I feel it's inadequate to think of art as useless, unless we're willing to go all the way. All the way in or all the way out, and this film feels like someone going all the way in to see what's there.

It's an art that's so grand that it feels comfortable to look at it with pity, a space where an artist puts everything in front of you and takes that gesture quite seriously, and your reaction to it—like any reaction to any vulnerability—inevitably communicates the most about where you're at, and that's okay, too.

I've just watched the ninth minute one more time, from a few seconds before to a few seconds after, and I think there's something to watching or taking in certain works of art in this manner. For some people, *S.N.Y.* is too much to bear in its entirety all at once. I don't know why I'm that sort of person, but I think it's true. Looking at this, though, and thinking about the whole of it, and what I like and dislike and love and hate about it, I'm certain it's a work of art. I used to say that *Paris, Texas* was my favorite film. Probably, in part, because I thought this made me sound cooler than I am, and partly because, when I first watched it, about forty minutes in, the sentence "this is my favorite film" came into my mind. It's odd because I don't sit around excited to watch that film, and I doubt I've even seen it more than ten times, but it's similar to *S.N.Y.* in that I know it affects me deeply, and there's something in it that resonates so much with me that I actually find it hard to watch. I have no doubt that Wenders' film would lend itself quite well to this sort of viewing experience. Piecemeal, split up, with the pressure lessened. I don't know what any of this means.

Minute 10

We get to fully see Caden at work now, directing his production of *Death of a Salesman*, and the shift in his demeanor fleshes out his character. At home, he's a mumbling, sad presence, quite used to being ignored. At the doctor's office, he behaves as if he's closer to being on equal footing, but this only leads to his butting heads with the doctors, who feel Caden is below them. At work, though, in the theater, with perhaps the most vulnerable version of human actors, he finally seems to possess the full weight of what he's decided is an ideal for living, for existence. Acting, in turn, is a curious thing, because from outside it can seem a ridiculous, cringey art form, and depictions of the theater in most any film or TV show haven't done much to alter this perception. Cassavetes, Fosse, though absolutely exceptions to this rule, are working against a tidal wave of "theater kid" tropes that prove difficult to live down.

In *S.N.Y.*, Kaufman's contribution to the enterprise is to treat it as a form of work. For every second we might see of actors acting, or Caden giving notes—in this scene he directs the young man playing Willy Loman about his sense of the fundamental catastrophe of living (he's using young actors in his production, setting his work apart)—we get a second, if not more, of stage managers, production designers resetting, building, or conversations between, about nothing much at all. I was tempted to say that at the center of it all Caden's genius shines through, but I'm realizing this is simply the tidal wave of critical commentary pushing me toward such a statement, because Kaufman is not, it must be said, treading over the artist-genius ground here; or if he is, he's doing so in a manner that lets us understand that artist-geniuses are propped up, their work is unromantic and frequently pathetic, they are flawed, they have guts, bad hair, weird rashes, obsessions that are not cool, or cute, and they exist in context, among others, and these others are essential.

We see, too, the beginning of what's certainly an unfortunate cliché, wherein Caden ogles a worker at the theater, a girl who's reading serious literature, improving herself, and who dresses and appears a bit like a woman in an advertisement from the 1960s. It's a cliché, yes, but it's counterbalanced by Adele's acts throughout the film, and the way in which it's depicted. And, what's more, in depicting it as an awkward, pathetic, stilted, misunderstood thing, Kaufman is invested in dissecting the cliché for all it's worth.

Minute 11

Caden's awkward workplace interactions with the woman feel like the stuff of every workplace comedy, but then he calls his doctors, and then he's shown poking around in his stool with a spoon. The stool is strange, glossy, and blackish. Then he's in bed, telling Adele he thinks there's blood in his stool.

"That stool in your office?"

The dynamic with their therapist thereafter is just incredible.
She's so funny, egging them on constantly. They're discussing
the aftermath of the birth of their daughter. Adele asks if she
can say something horrible, to which the therapist:

"Yes, please do."

Minute 12

There is a weird disparity between the compulsion to write
in a vulnerable—which is not the same as autobiographical—
manner, and the desired experience of then sharing this work
with someone, and more than this, of meaningfully offering
highly vulnerable emotional work to someone else. In the
apparatus of a narrative film, one can aspire toward catharsis
for an audience and for the creator of the work. One can aspire
to a satisfactory communication of anger. One can aspire to the
audience's vulnerable identification with our creations, or our
characters' apparent vulnerability, their sorrow, the awkward
shittiness of their reality, and so on. By embracing sorrow and

vulnerability, and some really ugly and simply sad moments in marriage and domestic life, and *not* resolving them toward catharsis, but instead leveling them at us and doubling down, it's a bit like moving beyond a state of fear to a state of anger. I remember once reading that the actor Christian Bale—who doesn't feature in *S.N.Y.*, but who strikes me as similarly mindful of his craft to Philip Seymour Hoffman—used to walk into this forest as a child, near his house, that terrified him. The idea was that he'd go directly at this thing that scared him most, at night, alone, and simply have done with it. To not only *call* the thing terrifying, but to immerse himself in it and get beyond that. Narrative film can do something similar. Give us something exact, ugly or awkward or sad or not, and then don't let it be vanquished by any hero. Instead, let the *hero's* apparent opposition, his hilariously biting and absurd therapist, tell him that his terrible feeling is good, and then cut back to his workplace, outside the theater, because inside it's a "nightmare."

Minute 13

There seems to need to be a meter in the contemporary filmmaker's head between total awkwardness and relief. I sometimes use Richard Linklater's film *Slacker* when I'm teaching, and in pretty much any context this is always something we get preoccupied with, where a scene could be so terribly uncomfortable, or a character so off-putting, that we'd just like to crawl out of our skin, and just then, when the tension of this total awkwardness is at its peak, that character will effectively drift out of the film forever, or if they return it's as a laughable afterthought, a background figure, dulled completely by whatever new context has been presented. Kaufman—and whether this has anything to do with his comedy background now strikes me as banal and uninteresting, so we'll stop—can be quite masterful at this, and yet there's still this wonderful discomfort that gets changed, because the things that seem to strike him as a voice in his movies as funny might be slightly off from those things most people readily find hilarious. Two people sit outside their workplace, discussing in vaguely flirty tones Franz Kafka's work, and because it's Kaufman we might briefly wonder whether we're going to gain some new insight into Kafka, because if anybody's going to weave that effectively into a character's neuroses, it'll be Kaufman; but all we get is the dull awkwardness of workplace flirtation, cranked up really high, if such a thing might be said, and a quick cut to an American plumber in an American T-shirt telling awkward theater director Caden Cotard he's "seen boy parts" in as disinterested a manner an American plumber might offer to dispel his worries over peeing being seen.

Minutes 14–15

We see Adele working—she's an artist too who paints tiny portraits. Caden isn't comfortable with the plumber and asks if he can take a piss in her sink, and Olive sits at the table between the two of them, she working and him pissing. It's a bit on the nose, but considering the eventual scale of Caden's work—and this can be delved into later—it's tempting to read into the fact that Adele is concerned with making something that's tiny and requires magnifying glasses to view, while Caden is concerned with the human scale, and eventually becomes concerned with the massive scale and the weird aporia this creates between the two of them. It's opening night, we find out, and Adele says she won't be able to attend, and because these two minutes flew weirdly by I'm skipping breaking them up, thinking instead about the movement from their home life, the lives of these two artists, to the actual opening of his rendition of *Death of a Salesman*, whose music we hear just at the end of this sequence.

I used to feel strange that so much of the art I was most invested in was art about artists and their lives in the midst of their making of art. I used to feel weird that it seemed as though the only people who ever reached out to me about my writing were writers themselves. I thought the goal was to reach "regular people," whatever that means. I can imagine Charlie Kaufman liking the idea of reaching these imagined people, at some point, but by the time of *S.N.Y.* I'd imagine his view of things had quite matured. I was a senior in high school when this film came out, and my mindset around the time would have been that any writing I did had to aspire to reach millions of people or it wasn't worth pursuing.

An interesting cultural development since 2008 has been the sheer number of people making art, and writing, and wanting to make art, and writing, and to be artists, and writers. This means that first I realized that for the most part they'd replaced "regular people" and to write things that engaged them would amount to about the same thing; and second, it forced me to realize that it didn't matter whether I was interested in watching films about filmmakers or artists, or writers, or writing things about the difficulty of writing things. If these were the places where my mind naturally seemed to drift when so prompted, then that was the long and the short of it, and that was where I should devote my focus. Kaufman's most recent film, *I'm Thinking of Ending Things*, which felt as though it contained a great energy but was unfortunately based on pretty cinematically limiting material—no shortage of irony that the comment in *Adaptation* about works about multiple personalities could now apply to one of Kaufman's films, though maybe Donald took over with *I'm Thinking of Ending Things*—featured one moment that really hit me hard when its protagonist essentially delivers a monologue/reading of a Pauline Kael review that, along with the musical numbers at the end, felt like Kaufman finally shining through after forcing himself to make a work for a time that felt outside his natural mode.

I applaud, as any fan of his would, his ambition to explore outside that natural mode. Kaufman's few recorded lectures on what he does are brilliant articulations of why this matters to him, and why it should matter to us, and why it simply matters, and probably the moments of pure Kaufman wouldn't have resonated so loudly had I not felt him making this awkward context work for the rest of it, but that was my experience.

I say all of this to say that, for the directions it will shortly go, *S.N.Y.*'s depictions of the lives of these artists are deeply moving. The theater pieces, the gallery showings, yes, but the small moments like a husband-director and a wife-artist having a difficult, across-the-chasm-of-their-misunderstanding conversation while the husband-director pees a disconcerting shade of brown into a basement sink and the wife-artist works intently at her tiny painting, a portrait of a naked woman sprawled on the corner of a bed. These small moments, showing the ways in which these people have had to adapt to live and to make their work, and how they've had to adapt to be married, and to be parents, strike me as one of the first examples of an American filmmaker in the twenty-first century taking up the mantle of Truffaut, of a human filmmaking that can still abrade, can hold its heavy hand at bay without losing its grip on the weird blemishes and tiny excesses that make these stories compelling.

Minute 16

In the notebook that Arthur Miller kept for *Death of a Salesman*, in his papers at the University of Texas at Austin, he wrote: "He who understands everything about his subject cannot write it. I write as much to discover as to explain."[3] In the sequence we get from the opening night for Caden's rendition of the play, we watch Willy Loman return home, and almost immediately cut to the after party, wherein Caden has a headache, and one of his actors—the fawning Claire, played by Michelle Williams—kisses him on the forehead and thanks him for his brilliance, apologizing for behaving like a baby. Someone, in passing, after Caden touches his aching head, says "Willy Loman!" which feels entirely like we're meant to see him as an extension of the character and which seems reasonable enough given S.N.Y's trajectory, and Miller's notion of the process of writing anything as one of discovery seems particularly essential to this iteration of Kaufman's output, wherein revisiting is constant, misunderstanding is constant, and our sense as an audience seems willfully thrown off by the creator of the work not simply to fuck with us, but to mine deeper into the particular well he's excavating through this character's head.

Minute 17

When I was younger and I'd watch this film I seemed to feel only a deep sorrow for its characters, and a discomfort, but it wasn't something I didn't like, because it was interesting. I do fundamentally believe that the artist ought to aspire to that one thing: to be interesting. I believe that Charlie Kaufman aspires always to be interesting, and that this carries him through everything wonderfully. It's hard to know whether I've sort of grown into S.N.Y., such that I no longer feel discomfort, or sorrow, for these people, but rather simply a kind of laughing love and distanced admiration for those similarly plighted, *lifed*, as it were, and not in need of any saving. Caden flirts awkwardly, again, with Hazel, the girl from work, at the after party while the two of them discuss getting high. It's really pathetic and wonderful, and the kind of thing you're not supposed to see up close.

Minute 18

This extends into the morning, and there's a moment that almost seems to reflect *The Last Supper*, where Caden is being held onto by Claire, and he has no twelve apostles, being a mere theater director in the aftermath of an after party, so he pokes noisily at the veins in his arm, and looks around, and asks nobody in particular when the reviews are going to get in. It's hard to imagine that such a world could exist, which brings me to another notion I couldn't shake while watching this film in a theater recently. The way Hazel approaches him, and Claire approaches him, I felt overwhelmed by this feeling of these being *projections* of Caden, things he *wanted* these people to be saying to him, rather than real things they were saying to him. Probably it connects with the dates, too, this sense that he is our protagonist, our anchor, as it were, and he doesn't even know the date, or the month, or potentially even the year, and these things are escaping him. The manner in which Hazel, or Claire flirts with Caden just feels so fantastical, and as it's happening they're seemingly so cut off from surrounding events, and it simply makes me curious to think what it might mean if this is intended in the film somehow, given what happens as it goes on, and his weirdly indifferent yet "maniacal" control over so many human figures enacting versions of so many human experiences. It isn't that Caden just doesn't register as a figure who'd beg such attentions. He's not a bad-looking person, though he's certainly an average, middling sort of suburban father, and seems constantly to be fretting over the edges of his skin. But he is this theater director, and in this context, with these people, this matters, and thus it's entirely possible, but the manner in which some people in the film talk with him makes it feel as though we're simply in his head, even though we're not exactly in his head. With the close of this minute Caden returns to find Adele is still awake, talking with her friend, Maria, and there's a bit of bitterness in the air. It's strange, too, these people—I'd imagine they're in their forties—existing in this weird, twenty-something way, staying out all night, and so on. They're artists, the thinking goes, which I do like. I don't like the direction it takes, not in terms of what I'd personally *prefer*, or argue for, and not in terms of what might have pushed back against the tendency in films about men and women and films about artist men and women, but that's alright, because I can see why Kaufman made the choices he made, and it makes sense. But there is this impasse, again, between Caden and Adele, and in this morning after moment, when none of them have slept, its name could be Hazel, could be Claire, could be Maria, but really it simply seems to be the long stretch of difficulty their marriage has faced, and the realization of something not apparent any longer for at least one of them.

Minute 19

This is the continuation of the inciting difficulty in their relationship, Caden's and Adele's, but really we have the sense that this is something that has been ongoing for months or years, however long these lives have collided with one another. This is distilled into a moment between a husband and a wife after the husband has finally shared this project he's been working at—and of course while he's working he's flirting and freaking out about illness and doing all of these other things that this particular iteration of the artist-husband does—and there may be expected this warranted antipathy based on the fact that Adele did not attend, and this is hinted at by Caden's "You're *stoned . . .*" as he makes his way up the stairs and away from Maria and Adele, but even this is not the petty bloodsport of early relationships. They are firmly in the middle or late-middle of their marriage, and have been for some time. They are firmly *both* artists, and while it *could* be said that each of their modes of art-making is approached in the manner of their gendered expectation, as characters in a film, this is simultaneously undercut in both directions by Adele's "bravado" and Caden's meek, pleasing manner.

Like the night before, when Caden and his cast and crew seemed like teenagers, Adele and Maria seem like teenagers now, high after staying up all night on the couch, talking, laughing, enjoying one another's company.

Minute 20

Synecdoche, New York directed by Charlie Kaufman © Sony Pictures Classics 2008. All rights reserved.

The music of *S.N.Y.* varies here between what I think of as the music of campus films—pulsating strings with long serious stretches and high crescendos of apparent achievement—with a more ominous, Hitchcock register lending if not menace then at least the sense of movement to the scene. We cut to Hazel driving, with neither Caden nor Adele nor anyone else around, which is nice, another way in which it isn't simply another Genius film. She's looking for a house to live in, we find, and approaches a bright yellow one with a realtor's sign out front, an ongoing house fire upstairs that no fire department tends to, that's addressed matter-of-factly by Hazel—"especially with the fire and all," she says—that's a moment, not unlike the opening of the suitcase in *Pulp Fiction*, or its progenitor in the Macguffin of *The 39*

Steps, that quickly sends people to Reddit seeking answers. Kaufman, in an interview, put it thusly:

> Well, she made the choice to live there. In fact, she says in the scene just before she dies that the end is built into the beginning. That's exactly what happens there. She chooses to live in this house. She's afraid it's going to kill her but she stays there and it does. That is the truth about any choice that we make. We make choices that resonate throughout our lives.[4]

Others have connected it to Tennessee Williams' line, that "We all live in a house on fire, no fire department to call; no way out, just the upstairs window to look out of while the fire burns the house down with us trapped, locked in it."[5]

What's interesting to me is, in my memory of the film, the fire was always small, and upstairs, and depicted in total darkness. In rewatching it I'm always surprised that it's first shown in broad daylight, in the awkward discourse of engaging with a realtor, and furthermore I'm always so uncomfortable realizing how abundant the smoke is throughout the house, as if it puts Hazel into a kind of living death. It's weird, because there are times when the burning house is played for humor, as in the interaction here, but it becomes this really tragic, heavy presence, where she's made this arbitrary choice, based on any number of factors, and it's slowly killed her. It used to comfort me to think of the Williams quote, that Kaufman was herein tying his film to Tennessee Williams' spirit, the same spirit Caden, and Hazel, and everyone wind up embracing. I don't feel bothered by that reading, and think really the film allows for it as much as anything, but when I was finally able to watch the film in a theater I couldn't believe how starkly bright it all was, how *bare*, and vulnerable, and sad. In a way it renders Hazel's character, and what she'll become in the artwork over the course of *S.N.Y.*, quite well. This closeness to this potentially threatening, bothersome, pathetic but maybe beautiful thing, a place to live her life, a room of her own, and it needn't be given some explanation, and why it can't simply be put out needn't be given some explanation. To simply let the thing exist for its own sake feels sufficient, while also feeling strangling.

Minute 21

"It's a big decision, how one prefers to die." There's a seamless transition between Derek, the son of the realtor who lives in the burning house, to the evening's second performance of *Death of a Salesman*, with Maria sitting between Caden and Adele, and Michelle Williams on stage performing as Claire Keen performing as Linda Loman, stretched out on the ground and unable to cry. If there's a cleanness to films, or filmmaking, that trims away the edges of living, there's an apparent interest in *S.N.Y.* and in Kaufman to hold onto as much of what's unclean as possible, to move between what we know is an ordered, directed scene involving a woman looking for a house, and a more ordered, more directed scene within a theater stage within a scene within a film, but without making it hyper-stylized, and instead making it mournful, so that the sad emotions Hazel experiences segue into the sad emotions of Linda Loman, without losing our interest and without preaching, or bemoaning these sadnesses. We don't feel overwhelmed, or even necessarily sad ourselves. We can simply bask in something other than we'd expected.

Minute 22

There's a weird and abrupt shift in the tenor of their conversation as they leave the theater. Caden and Adele are up front, briefly fielding questions from Caden's parents, and compliments from Maria, when Adele critiques the whole thing, saying he's simply restaging someone else's work, for "blue-

haired regional theater subscribers." It's night, and the whole
scene feels as if it's shot by Gordon Willis, and it's clear that
Caden might want to fight back—he states, noncommittally,
that people were leaving the theater crying—but that he's
also taking in what Adele is saying, and that this might be
a pivotal moment for him, a critique he's taking to heart
from someone whose opinion on these matters he respects,
though obviously it's got to hurt him. There is also the obvious
question of whether Kaufman himself might have felt like this
in his career, having made films that were originals, working
under other directors, and adaptations, working under other
directors. Though not quite the same thing as restaging Arthur
Miller, as well-trod a playwright one is likely to find short of
Shakespeare, it does seem worth considering the trajectory of
Kaufman's career, arriving at *S.N.Y.*, and what he does when he
finally has total control. At a minimum this moment embodies
a frustration, and it's a frustration familiar to anyone who has
read or watched or listened to Kaufman talk anywhere. You
try, and you try, and you try; and the end result is affected
by vague things outside of your control; and then you try in
that new context, and finally whether all that trying is even
witnessed comes down to *money*. For Caden, he thought he
was doing something significant with *Death of a Salesman*,
not just in terms of the younger actors, but the staging itself. At
the end, when Linda's on Willy's grave, we face the reality that
he's been limited by the context he tried to force his expression
into, and really, if Adele had simply done her supposed duty,
and praised the play, and continued on, he would have been
worse off; we can feel this. There's concern, too, about the
fact that time is running out, that Caden's getting old, and he
might want to work more aggressively to find the thing he
wants said. Though we know the narrative doesn't sustain
their relationship, their love life, then, we can understand this
as an act of love. It's certainly the act that sets in motion the
real guts of *S.N.Y.*

Minute 23

The morning that opens the film is more or less repeated here, excepting the new presence of Caden's father sleeping on the couch, or what appears to be Caden's father, and new complaints of arthritis from Caden, or possible arthritis, and Olive is already eating and watching cartoons, while Adele sits on the phone, and we're not sure who she's talking to, but it seems clear enough it's Maria, which is shortly confirmed, and Caden gruffly states "it's been three hours since you spoke." Again, we see the newspaper, the front page, which now states *MAY 25, 2006*, which taken at face value means it's been a year since the film started, or maybe slightly more, or maybe slightly less. Adele, we hear, is going to Berlin, and wants to go there with only Olive, and we see the beginnings of a real change between Caden and Adele, which doesn't feel heartbreaking so much as businesslike, an agreement, and neither party seems particularly exhilarated by the prospect, though certainly Adele seems to feel some sense of enacting a more ideal existence than what she's been experiencing. When Caden states "My joints are stiff," Adele pauses before taking a slow sip of her coffee, staring off and taking in what's been said in only the way a spouse who's long been in the trenches of marriage and parenting can. What's nice is it's not snarky, it's not *annoyed*, really, so much as just accepting. The tragedy of all of our lives will keep happening to us whether we accept it or not.

Minute 24

The trip to Berlin is seemingly decided by Adele, though for Caden, and for us, by extension an unease has started to bloom. Caden wonders why, and the thing is largely left off before Caden heads out—we don't see this—and walks Olive to school. He's growing pustules on his face now, and wasn't,

I don't think, growing them previously. "It's called sycosis," he says, attempting to be a useful father, offering some sort of information out of his unfortunate state of suffering to his curious and vocal daughter. Although they *aren't* parents that homeschool, their house feels more lived-in than some, perhaps because they're artists. We homeschool, in the aftermath of Covid, and what with school shootings and the like, it just seemed like the thing to do. My wife does the majority of it, and I'll often have moments like this, where a curiosity from my oldest daughter, or my son, or my youngest daughter, will ask about something, and I'll heap on information, excited that I actually have something to offer in them. It's just hit me, however, that some of what Caden's doing might be in anticipation of what's about to happen, Adele leaving for Berlin for however long—as the film plays out the trip becomes much longer, but part of me likes the idea that the film is actually just about the hell father-husbands can get into when wife-mothers go away for a few days on trips with the kids. He's not sure where this change is coming from, this new decision, and the stuff with Maria, and the sense of their marriage on the rocks, so he wants to offer his daughter something substantial, and perhaps, too, the talk from Adele, the idea that he doesn't have forever to decide what he wants to leave behind as an artist, is affecting him. So he offers her a distinction between "psychosis" and "sycosis," and it is good.

Minute 25

Almost instantly we're back inside with only Adele and Caden, in their bedroom, and Caden asks if he's disappointed her somehow. Catherine Keener's interesting to me because I can remember being reminded of certain people I knew when I was younger when I watched films involving her, and at the time it bothered me. I was literally a teenager, and thinking probably of scratchy-voiced moms of friends, and so on, and thus as I've grown older I've had to accept that this is not something to base a fundamental opinion of an actor on; yet it wasn't until I first watched *Capote* that her real necessity as an actor struck me, and it's frankly astounding thinking that Bennett Miller's masterful film also starred Philip Seymour Hoffman, and was made only a couple of years apart from *S.N.Y.* In terms of magnitude, it's as astounding as the fact that *Jurassic Park* and *Schindler's List* were made by the same director within the same calendar year. We've had the sense throughout the opening here that Adele is ready to move on, and possibly even a bit indifferent to the inevitable suffering that will ensue when she's left. I don't mean she's seemed cold, because that's cliché, and she has not. She's seemed overwhelmed, rather, whenever dealing with her actually overwhelming existence, and the only times she hasn't seemed overwhelmed have been when she's been with Maria; but of course this is the thorny stuff of leaving one relationship, one marriage, for another. The weight of it hits her after she tries to do the cool, dismissive artist thing of questioning "romantic-love," and she sits on the bed to cry, to apologize to Caden, to cry.

Minute 26

After the tears, things become businesslike again, and we then weirdly cut to an advertisement for "Flurostatin TR," a drug for those going through chemotherapy. We cut from this to a shot of Caden, seated, watching a TV set, which is old, brushing his teeth in his underwear and a shirt, picking at a scab at his leg as he notices himself put into the ad, running in a park and smiling with the others in the advertisement. It seems very important that Caden have Philip Seymour Hoffman's physical body at this point in the film. I can remember, not unlike the experience of seeing Catherine Keener when I was younger and dumber, wondering at times why an actor like Philip Seymour Hoffman might be cast in a major role in a film. Not actually wondering, really, so much as simply feeling strange that he was featured so prominently, and that his body never seemed to get into the shapes of other actors, and his awkwardness, his doughiness, felt strange opposite Tom Cruise, for instance, in the third installment of the new *Mission Impossible* franchise. I didn't even think these things, really, I simply felt them, and that was that. Some actors will make me uncomfortable with the stubbornness with which they'll cling to badly taken care of bodies. I don't necessarily look at Hoffman as having a badly taken care of body, though. He has the thoroughly middling body of a well-to-do father and husband. He's not even really obese, or if he is, medically speaking, he's not the kind of obese that should cause people alarm. He looks as though he doesn't say no to snacks, because he's in pain at being alive yet more. He looks as though he eats what his kids don't eat when they've finished with dinner. This is, for the most part, and for what it's worth, what I look like. At this point, though, in this film, when doing things like showering, for Caden, must feel rather silly, because in a way his heart has been ripped out of his chest and taken to Germany—and yet he must shower, because that is what the living do, they shower—his physical presence could not be more apt, more perfect, more fitting. He sits in average-looking clothes, watching an ad that's suddenly featuring himself, and perhaps he's hallucinating, perhaps he's simply overly fixated on medical problems; it almost doesn't seem to matter *why*, we just know that we are benefited as viewers if we can empathize with this presence, and hold to him.

Minute 27

All of us in the theater were relieved to see the therapist again. This is not so easy as it seems. The heavier your subject matter, the better fit the comic relief needs to provide. If you go too dark—or really "too dark" isn't the phrase, rather *very dark*—then things open up, and you're again able to simply offer dumb dick and/or fart jokes, like in most every horror film or action film. In a film like this, though, where we've seen, or we're probably at least vaguely familiar with *Being John Malkovich*, and *Adaptation*, and *Eternal Sunshine of the Spotless Mind*, we go in not necessarily thinking about laughter, though certainly those films afford us bits of laughter here and there, most especially in the cases of the former two, which are probably the better of the three together. We also quickly enter the consciousness of a man so besotted with such an everyday kind of misery, worry, sorrow, and medicalized paranoia that to simply escape it with some bit loud fart would somehow jar too much, so the therapist made us laugh a really gut-level laugh, and warm up again to what was coming. And yes, and yes, out, damn spot, Caden is Lady Macbeth. Caden is facing the guilt he feels for all of it.

Minute 28

Perhaps, because the compaction of sorrow in *S.N.Y.* is one of its strengths—every sorrowful aspect is purely rendered, compressed, like a diamond—and because Caden might have felt these things, tidied up, sat watching the advertisement, over a year, or a day, or a month, there's justification for some relief, which we receive by going out into the world. First to the therapist, who sells Caden the book she's written, *Getting Better*, which he finds he's anticipatorily endorsed when viewing her website later on, and then to the dentist, who quickly, as only doctors and dentists and probably lawyers—fingers crossed—can do, returns the man back to the living: "Some fives. That's not good." I'll admit that I've for the majority of my life been an awful patient for these people, and thus I know this disappointment as well as anything—too well—and yet because they never get the hint, they never simply reschedule on a monthly basis, or establish a mode of being wherein I want to return with any frequency, by the time it's time for the appointment again—for Caden it could have been a decade, we just can't be sure—I've completely forgotten how pathetic and childlike I'll feel when they start to list out their (my/Caden's) numbers.

Minute 29

As they're wont to do, the dental appointment becomes a periodontal appointment, at which point Caden's gums are operated on, violently bloodying the inside of his mouth. Then he's back at home, on a Nokia cellphone calling Adele, who's in Berlin—it sounds like she's surrounded by people—and she can't really hear Caden—she thinks it's Ellen—and Caden tells her he can't wait to see her and Olive on the 12th, but really it sounds as if the matter of their marriage is already settled, behind them, more in line with what we'd imagined Adele's perspective to be on the whole thing before her weeping, her breaking down. This too lends itself to the notion that some of this is the result of Caden's head, or that this is a dark rendering of what goes through the father-husband's psyche when the family takes a trip without him. Of course this is only my own response, but the extremity to which he quickly dips or rises seems wholly to support it. After hanging up the phone, or being hung up on rather, by Adele—who laughs and says she's famous!—Caden begins to seize, but it's a weird sort of seizing, like he's a child faking sick, but there's an interesting dimension here—why shouldn't a person be capable of *choosing to seize?*—where his hypochondria becomes *active*, or perhaps now it's fully Munchausen, which I think would fit because there is no "by proxy," it's him seemingly enacting this upon himself. Perhaps, though, he's really seizing, and I just identify with Caden too much, and I can imagine myself dramatically having a pretend seizure and calling 911 and screaming "I'm sick! I'm sick!" a little too easily.

Minute 30

Every hospital is housed in a decrepit basement, or—and how would you put this?—every hospital *is* a decrepit basement, for Mr. Cotard. There are magazines, though! The magazines, however, contain depictions of Adele, now ridiculously successful as an artist, surrounding herself with "joyous" people, *thriving*, while Mr. Cotard wallows in the decrepit basement, led one way by a staff member and then weirdly jolted from this route by the doctor who randomly opens a door while the staff member walks off—it's funny, it's funny— and we're informed he's had "a seizure, of sorts," and maybe this is why I've felt so skeptical of this aberration, although probably it's really only me, and my projecting, and that is that.

Minute 31

"How to Not Be a Perfectionist
People are vivid
and small
and don't live
very long—"

                                        (*Molly Brodak, entire poem*)

We are all of us going to die. This is inescapable. How we respond to this reality is one of the ways we begin to make meaning within our lives. For Caden, and presumably by extension Kaufman, this becomes enacted in the interactions we have, the moments of love, the awkward aspirings toward love, any gesture we might make to realize this—and then our art, which has happened for Caden and which is forthcoming in extremis—and so the bad news from the doctor almost doesn't seem to matter, and so the meeting with Hazel can now seem changed, and so the sorrow we might rightly be feeling from Adele and Olive being gone is still sorrow, but can perhaps be quieted or connected with something larger, some tangible tether to our humanity. *I'm just a little person . . . A person, in a sea . . .*

Minute 32

There is sorrow and there is warmth, or rather, there is the potential for sorrow and the potential for warmth, in every human face and every human interaction. Caden and Hazel, and Adele is gone, in Berlin, for perhaps a week, for perhaps a year, we can't be sure which of these two we might feasibly trust, and really it doesn't seem important any longer. There is this warm moving now, a flow, everything flows, everything passes. It isn't as though he's holding onto youth, because that isn't what's happening. It isn't as though she's desperately clinging to something, because that isn't what's happening. The two of them are perfect beings, embroideries of human being, of life and of experience, and both of them are merely trying, trying, to ensue, to persist, to go on.

Minute 33

The burning of Hazel's house is now a comfort, such that the entire place now feels like the inside of a smoking hearth, an inversion of the massive fireplace at the end of *Citizen Kane*, when the world has gotten quite cold, and everything is splitting. Hazel is in the powerful position now and can relish the experience, and Caden, in the glaring light of his reality, is discomfited, but seemingly because of his guilty nature, his shamed or shameful nature, he doesn't resist when she tells him what to do, though the thing quickly gets to that uncomfortable place of pornography, the language of pornography, someone suddenly and glaringly called "Baby" can wield so much obscenity, and the warmth of the burning house can only slightly hold the beauty of the moment there, the smoke of the room causing a nice haze which we needn't notice is poisonous.

Minute 34

Though it starts to fall apart, the moment becomes punctured and Caden disappoints and Hazel becomes disappointed when they begin to fuck, the music because it persists allows this to become another part of this larger flowing presence, the watery nature of the movie, where perhaps we've been suddenly plopped in a disappointing tidepool, surrounded by sharp black rocks, but the sun still blares down, and we can feel its presence. This kind of disappointment, this overthinking in the practice of sex, and the concurrent shift that happens between both parties, the shame and the disappointment on the one hand, and the frustration and beginnings of inward doubting and disappointment on the other, might have been the kind of thing I'd thought a filmmaker could only superficially touch, but here it's as if the music, a simple and yet not cheesy bar jazz song about loneliness and the simple world, with piano and lightly brushed drums, accounts for the feelings of both Hazel and Caden, and allows for both of them, what they're experiencing, such that the awkwardness of it can in fact turn into something quite beautiful.

Minute 35

Time is a frankly violent thing in life, and I'm tempted to say not in this film, but then I'd only be glorifying my sufferings over the sufferings of what I'm assuming cannot have been particularly well-paid actors; though of course they made do, of course they must have been OK, though for how long on only the paycheck from it is tough to say. What the film communicates is the violence of time in the mind of the viewer, rather than *depicting* this violence, but here again, I cannot tell whether I'm glorifying my own experiences over the fictive experiences wrought from someone's head and put into existence on screen. It seems patently obvious, too, that time is a violent thing to the characters in this film. Doesn't it? Doesn't Caden experience time as a violent thing? Is he depicted in such a way that time for him is violent? This is where I veer. Most of the time it's treated as a foible, or depicted as a foible, as a small quirk of the universe for these people, but at the same time it's treated differently over the course of the film, that is, our sense of it becomes quite heavy and quite tragic, such that by the end we only wish to utter that final word and join Caden in the long sleep. I do not think that Charlie Kaufman set out to enact in the minds of his viewers this notion of time being a violent thing, and I do not think that he set out to convey time as this really oppressive entity in our lives, though now that I've written that out, it seems quite plausible; the latter, that is, and not the former. Caden fails and then sits on the stairs in his empty home like a teenager calling the girl with whom he failed. She's now indifferent. He'd said the wrong thing, and more than that, said "just the wrong thing to say right now," which anybody who's ever said such a thing knows, closes a door forever, and to close a door in a house whose upstairs is constantly on fire is simply no good; it simply will not do. Nobody can wallow in the richness of an impasse between two human beings like Kaufman. If there's anything to say of him, it's that. We feel every crawling awkwardness on the physiques of Caden and Hazel as they're laid out in their beds in much the same way we get into every minutia of a Gregory Crewdson photograph once it's hooked us; this little domestic event becomes a crime scene, every bead of sweat a possible point of interest, every grimace a burrow into which the whole of light is plugged.

Minute 36

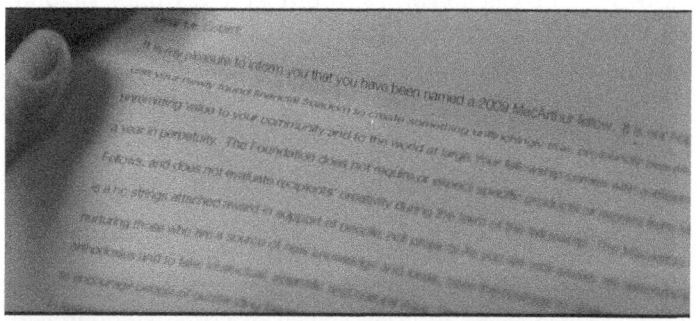

"Correspondence"
Caden receives a fax from Adele in Berlin asking Caden not to
read Olive's diary per Olive's wishes, and basically instantly
this sends Caden to Olive's room where he grabs the diary,
and it's not the kind of thing it typically is, because given
the circumstances on Olive's side it's understandable, that is,
she's just a kid, has a random thought, sees Mom sending
a fax or something, and makes sure to tell him not to read
it; but the reality of this narrative is important, given how
close it sometimes gets to seemingly not being invested in
this reality, and yet the film does hinge on us being able to
accept that these fictional depictions of people matter, these
characters matter. The reality for Caden is he hasn't seen his
wife or daughter for weeks, perhaps a year, perhaps longer,
they are gone. What's more, the world has been telling him
strange things, sending him strange signals, and this might
be one sure tether to something meaningful from what might
be considered his old life—in many ways his real life, or the
Real. Before he can wade into the diary just yet there's a
knock at the door, and an envelope is handed to Caden, and
again reality becomes vitally important to *S.N.Y.*, an entity

or an event from reality becomes essential, the MacArthur Genius Grant, which any living American artist is probably aware of, and which many of us probably yearn for any time we hear of its existence again. The film more or less opens with Harold Pinter winning the Nobel Prize in Literature, so the actual lives of successful or unsuccessful artists are very much a part of what Kaufman is telling us in *S.N.Y.* "It is our hope that you will use your newly found financial freedom to create something unflinchingly true, profoundly beautiful and of unremitting value," the letter states, and Caden quickly confers with the therapist in the aftermath, avowing that he's going to make a theater piece, something in line with what Adele seemed to be accusing Caden of not attempting with his restaging of *Death of a Salesman*. I admit that there have been stretches of my existence where I've considered writing, art-making, filmmaking, art of any kind really, to be a largely solitary endeavor, excepting of course group artworks, though even in the case of these I'd typically argue that one person was largely in control. What I like about this is it basically immediately undercuts the idea of Genius, that the Writer-Genius is a quiet sufferer alone in a room, and so on. These people certainly exist, but they are served in some capacity by others, their work is supported in some sense by others, even if those others are their dead parents, leaving them enough money to exist alone and write and worry over little else. Caden immediately sees his therapist after winning a grant that largely frees him up to do just about anything he'd like to do as an artist. Clearly he's aware of his vulnerability, but clearly Kaufman too is aware of depicting an artist-"genius" of a stripe that runs counter to the majority of narratives about these people we've received. His role as a theater director, rather than a poet, or visual artist, seems to be the first iteration of this, because to do his most satisfactory work he must work with others, but this is only one aspect of Caden's reliance on others to live, and hence to do his most satisfactory work. The doctors, the therapists, the friends, the family, the MacArthur organization, any success in any artist's life takes a village, and this is more beautiful, *S.N.Y.* seems to argue, than solitary figures laboring in quiet rooms.

Minute 37

Part of the problem of the artist is the disparity between living largely in fabricating an idealized world. Even in the case of the purely abstract sculptor, the idea of bringing something forth into the world is tied to vision, to imagining, and this is probably why so many artists struggle with the basic shit of living, that is, they're either being encouraged, or they're encouraging themselves in spite of the world's seeming active discouragement, to make this work that is not obviously saleable, not obviously useful, not obviously popular, and which in terms of the walking populace of human beings does not "need" to be made, but they feel what's very often a dire conviction of its necessity—they are not fucking around, it is not a mere thing, any hobby—and yet the world does not, especially now, and certainly just several years ago when *S.N.Y.* was made, conform in any manner to their vision of it. The MacArthur Grant is referred to as the "Genius Grant," and Caden says he wants to earn it to his therapist. She immediately tells him about a brilliant novel, written by a four-year-old who committed suicide at five, called *Little Winky*, who's "a virulent antisemite." There is much to be taken from this reality, the notion that we are never really going to be this idealized thing, because every week another one comes along more perfectly embodying the bright young genius. There is only the work, then, and if we forgo this we're really fucked. It reminded me, too, of Earl Mac Rauch's brilliant novel *Dirty Pictures from the Prom*, written when he was young, wherein a young man, who wants to be an artist, has a brother who I believe was fresco painting the floor of their garage, before committing suicide at I think the age of eight, and his talent is overshadowing anything the brother might do. Certainly Oscar Wilde had something to say about all of this, but maybe I'm misremembering.

Minute 38

For a beautiful fleeting instant we get to see Caden in the throes of his inspiration over the reception of the grant, and his ideating over the prospect of his piece, his theater piece, when he's taken to look at the cavernous warehouse in which he'll build his masterpiece. He's energized, seemingly, but skeptical at first—"Plays?" [. . .] "Like, theater plays?"—and yet the absurd notion of conducting his work inside this cavernous space, seemingly the size of a small town, takes on a quick logic when balanced against the sort of torpor of everything that's preceded it, the loss, the depression, but more exactly the daily sorrow of being this artist and failing in small, simple ways throughout each moment, simply being a person and failing, simply being a dad, a father, and failing, simply being a husband and losing what's what. And then another recognizable setup: when you've lost most of everything, and offended even those with whom you've engaged in a prolonged dalliance that you direly botch, and you're given a massive grant of lots of money, and you're really ideating, the person with whom you've exchanged this dalliance is going to be as indifferent to you as the cactus is to the random neon-covered hiker; loud and excited and inspired though you may be in what you're doing, try persisting in such a state, in your toxic environment, starved of the kinds of things that give one life, and getting excited because somebody's flaunting their money.

Minute 39

Without simply wanting to diverge into the throes of a depressive soap opera, Kaufman thwarts our hero by revealing his medical condition has made it such that he can hardly swallow anything, and must summon his spit before eating like a ridiculous square-jawed bull; and what's more, we're now going to get to watch this guy eat a bowl of soup— somehow, somehow—in a diner across from this woman, this muse, after delivering a monologue about enacting a theater piece allowing both audience and performer to bask "in the very menstrual blood" of their creation. Although comedy can sometimes cheapen things that aspire to really do something—especially when that "something" is the life and lifework of a purportedly brilliant artist—the comedy in this moment is so strangely set up, and at every degree of separation—Hoffman and Morton to Kaufman to Kafka to Shakespeare to the Old Testament and further—so richly and humanly embarrassing that it feels like the comedy in life, the final belly laugh after the long and stressful day assembling the bunk bed, the noxious and horrific fart of the kid in the tent on the miserable camping trip.

Minute 40

Here we really get to see the ritual of eating, when Hoffman/ Caden takes a spoonful of soup into his mouth, and sort of holds it there, mouth slightly downward, and raises his head several times, almost as if he's trying to prepare to lob a ball over a wall or something, using his lips to fling the spoonful of soup up past his uvula and over the wall down into his esophagus, after which he tilts his head up, swallowing oddly, and continues entirely straight-faced and committed to recruiting Hazel to his endeavor, and her response is not some seething tirade; she simply says she's not sure she could work with him, that she's pretty mad, and what's still more funny is she seems surprised by this, as if she hadn't really given the matter much thought, but yeah, *yeah*, in a way what he'd done really irked her. Caden's response, that he's "just trying to normalize it," is aspirationally peppy, as if the rising tide of the grant and this work is sufficient to get any and all around him above this muck, but he feels in this moment more like an aloof physician, like those we've previously seen in *S.N.Y.*, unaware of the emotional tenor of any situation because the money is finally right and the work must get done. We then get a shift to the more lowing piano music, resounding sadly when Caden finally plucks open Olive's diary, alone in her room, and reads the childlike scrawl of her introduction, that her favorite color is pink, which sends him quickly to the store where a clerk lifts a large pink box onto the counter featuring a simple illustration of the outline of a nose, over which is printed the word: "Nose." I can picture the three of them, Caden's back facing the camera to the right, the clerk facing Caden and our direction in the middle, and the large, pastel-pink box, none of it really making much sense at all, but her delivery is razor sharp: "This is pink," and the idea of shipping this, of all things, to a small child in Berlin with her mother the artist and her lover, and what in god's name she'll do with it, sort of warms the heart.

Minute 41

Caden ships the package to Olive, a box wrapped up in box-colored paper, that is the brown packing paper, or a box inside of a box, I'm uncertain. Then we're in the sort of locker room

of the warehouse, where he's gathered a massive number of
people for the production he's beginning, and he begins with
them by telling them that they'll begin "by talking honestly,"
and the room suddenly takes on the aura of an AA meeting,
and it's striking me the real rarity of such a situation, the rarity
of an artist like this, who really doesn't ever appear "cool,"
and doesn't appear to be struggling in a kind of Beethovian
manner, or like Pollock, or any of these figures we've so
romanticized from history. He looks simple, and sort of small,
and timid, sitting before them, like we all usually look in an
AA meeting, or an NA meeting, or any place we've gone to
find religion in this post-religion moment we're presently
crawling, struggling through as a population. For Caden,
the thing is art, and by extension, I think for Kaufman, the
thing is art, and what's stirring about this moment is it's a
real depiction of this phenomenon, the same phenomenon
I think that David Foster Wallace was enacting when he
incorporated so much of recovery and AA into *Infinite Jest*.
The same experience, too, apparent in the "colifata" depicted
in Francis Ford Coppola's masterful *Tetro*, wherein a group of
patients at a mental health clinic and citizens in Buenos Aires
can gather together and speak into a circulated microphone
about their troubles, to have it broadcast on local radio. This
is based on an actual group, "LT 22 Radio 'La Colifata',", and
in *Tetro* it's the first moment we really get when our artist-
genius character can speak with relative comfort about what's
happening inside of him. Caden is like this, but realizes, too,
the necessity of this, the need *he* has for it, *and* these people,
to do something significant, and I think it's arguable Kaufman
realized it too, and probably realized it prior to this, hence the
vulnerability and autobiography of *Adaptation*. It isn't that
Caden, or Kaufman, or Wallace, or Don Gately, or "Tetro" are
simply selfish, needful of the spotlight on their works, their
sufferings, their heartache. It's that their present context has
become such an impossibility, and the usual ways of dealing
with it are so fraught and inaccessible if you're not born into
them—and most of them eventually run—and though I'm sure

there's temptation to simply flee and awkwardly lob alcohol up into his throat on a Mexican beach until he's dead, he does the thing the artist feels compelled to do with the money he's given; he sets something up without total certainty as to where it's going, but he commits himself to it so that these others are able to commit in turn. He works.

Minute 42

What, in the end, does an artist have to offer the world? What is the summation of their work? It must vary—I'm certain it must vary. From William Gaddis to Jim Thompson there's much variation. I prefer Jim Thompson and think that I'm right. Caden says that we are all going to die and that we all secretly believe that we won't, and I don't think that I agree with this latter. Maybe it's generational. It's probably generational. An artist has only the entirety of their life and what they're able to put into it to offer the world. I get the sense that the early twentieth century is comprised of a mountain of these unsung works. The works being sung about are somehow beside the point. There are masterpieces of the week, works of genius of the week, and works of genius for the entirety of it, masterpieces for the entirety of time. Somebody said that, I think, on the Internet. Their talk continues, their beginning communing, and trying to figure it out, and Michelle Williams' Claire, in her earnestness, and the need to move from the pain of Caden's state to something redemptive is the perfect modeling of the critical process in so many cases. There is a work, a rawness, a person laying themselves sort of bare, and there is a human observing this person doing this, and if it doesn't get contextualized quickly we're simply going to lose it, to crawl out of our skin. Caden doesn't seem to want this, or would probably like to quiet Claire a bit, because she's certainly washing out whatever it is he's talking about, but at the same time there seems to be a desire for this to be a truly democratic work, not in any vile despicable political terms—that's not what this is for—but in terms of actually opening the work to every possible voice. In a way, then, *S.N.Y.* is a utopian work, a film that seeks to embrace contrary viewpoints, contrary even to the perspective of the creator, much as Caden's play is an unnamed play, featuring actors and production designers with radically different perspectives from him, who, when they offer suggestions, are usually incorporated into the work, but we're not there yet. Claire's contribution is not disputed or shouted down by another actor, which even in my tenth viewing I must have expected, it just seems right for it, but no, her presence is acknowledged, and what she has to contribute is included. And then, as we've tended to get thus far in moments when the tension rises, we shift to something immensely pleasant, a sort of Abbot and Costello-style bit where Caden sees Hazel and the boy living in her basement where he's out for dinner, seemingly waiting for someone, and when he sees them enter, he ducks his head down at the table, and of course then the person he's waiting for shows up. First, though, we do get a small critique of Claire, or at least it's what I'd call it, where she sees Hazel and can't for the life of her remember her name, and then remembers her role at the box office, acknowledges this, and they start to idly chat. An artist can only really offer their attempts; in the end, that is the thing they fundamentally have to offer. They offer their attempts, which fail, or are perceived to fail, or succeed, or are perceived to succeed, both by the audience and the artist, and then time comes into it, and history, and context, and analysis, and throughout all of it we have these simple human figures trying, trying, working toward something which they feel driven to attempt, and most of the time they might not even know why, but they need to act natural.

Minute 43

There is for the artist probably always this desire to hide and to recoil from the world, to shrivel up into our own quiet thing, which is not always the correct impulse, but which is often the thing that leads to work. Not having the option to do this in this case, because Caden has seemingly tasked himself with generating his masterpiece without sitting and writing it out in its entirety first, he becomes the goof, sure, but it isn't approached in a purely comedic way. It feels approached like Truffaut, where everyone's talk will get the thing across, each of these people, even Hazel's date, will move the scene from A to B in its weird and human stubbornness, though in this stretch it's smooth, and feels like the best of those moments in *Phantom Thread*, when Jonny Greenwood's music floods the image and we are quiet, and the talk of the characters might move within the music and without, or maybe Vertigo, where there should be at every edge the twitch of menace, the flickers of betrayal or the flashings of sudden anger, but these are only hints, as Caden is only building, and Hazel is only considering, and Claire is only acting, and Derek is only tan. The scene's warm light, and the way the tufted leather booths the characters get lost in blend quite prettily with the ornate wallpaper, with the characters speaking just above a whisper in the full warmth of their breath, and the music pressed against this; the whole of it is perfect.

Minute 44

"I keep thinking about Artaud, Krapp's Last Tape, and, you know, Grotowski, for chrissake." (Claire)
"I don't know what I'm doing." (Caden)

"Why do we sacrifice so much energy to our art?

Not in order to teach others but to learn with them what our existence, our organism, our personal and repeatable experience have to give us; to learn to break down the barriers which surround us and to free ourselves from the breaks which hold us back, from the lies about ourselves which we manufacture daily for ourselves and for others; to destroy the limitations caused by our ignorance or lack of courage; in short, to fill the emptiness in us: to fulfill ourselves . . . art is a ripening, an evolution, an uplifting which enables us to emerge from darkness into a blaze of light."—Jerzy Grotowski[6]

"Here I end this reel. Box--(pause)--three, spool--(pause)--five. (Pause.) Perhaps my best years are gone. When there was a chance of happiness. But I wouldn't want them back. Not with the fire in me now. No, I wouldn't want them back.

Krapp motionless staring before him. The tape runs on in silence."—Samuel Beckett, *Krapp's Last Tape*[7]

"Theater of Cruelty means a theater difficult and cruel for myself first of all. And, on the level of performance, it is not the cruelty we can exercise upon each other by hacking at each other's bodies, carving up our personal anatomies, or, like Assyrian emperors, sending parcels of human ears, noses, or neatly detached nostrils through the mail, but the much more terrible and necessary cruelty which things can exercise against us. We are not free. And the sky can still fall on our heads. And the theater has been created to teach us that first of all."—*The Theater and Its Double*, Antonin Artaud[8]

While it is true that on the one hand *S.N.Y.* is not a film that resigns itself to mere referentiality, in largest part because Caden is a person who largely doesn't allow himself to be resigned to mere referentiality, these three referents struck me as pretty obviously significant on the one hand, while being maybe less obviously applicable to Kaufman if one hasn't picked any of them up. We know Artaud, probably, indirectly—we've seen his image, we've heard of his struggle—and Beckett, of course, but probably more for *Waiting for Godot* or the extremely spare prose than anything else. What's doubly interesting is Caden's disregard of this, and Kaufman behind it, seemingly on the one hand attempting to justify his work's existence (singular because I'm speaking of *S.N.Y.* in particular here, though it could apply to any reference across all of it), while also dismissing this tendency as a weakness, a flaw, an effort to excuse away what might be laziness or an inability to bring all of it together. Putting it into the voice of Claire of all the film's characters, too, aligns her with Hazel—and ironically here Claire is talking about aping Hazel at the beginning of developing her character, to which Caden failingly demurs—who reads and briefly dissects Proust and Kafka with Caden, but again in that case Caden's reaction is not to wax intellectually, but to speak in baser terms, largely guided by flirtation and self-doubt, that latter of which has overwhelmed the former in this case with Claire. I don't know what the ideal function of the reference in a fictive work is to be. In her *Essays One*, recently, I read Lydia Davis talk about a short story she'd written where she essentially tried to pepper a brief lesson in French, which is certainly a potential adjacent benefit to referentiality. It can, too, it should be said, function as a justification within the work, or a kind of inverse artist's statement through the voices of others for that which is being reached for. It can be a comment on our fragmented consciousness, which probably applies readily to *S.N.Y.*, since even beyond Kaufman's consciousness split across these stories and these characters as both director and as writer, we also have Caden as the director of Claire, the creator of this work, the person who probably put Claire in mind of these figures, or at least a contributing factor in her serious pursuit of acting, and part of the justification for her being put in mind of these figures. There are times, such as presently, in this brief section—potentially a small essay, a little world, at least that's how I sometimes like to think of them—wherein the thinking is pretty straightforward: they are just much better than my voice, what I might have to say about it, and I invoke them because they are the purest distillation of the idea I'd wish to touch.

KAUFMAN,   ARTAUD,   BECKETT,   GROTOWSKI.
WILLIAMS, SEYMOUR HOFFMAN, MORTON, SPARKS.

Minute 45

As they're walking to Claire's apartment, after dinner, Claire tells Caden that her mother died last night. Not having experienced this, I cannot attest to the strange experience the death of a mother can be, or the strange reaction we might have to such a thing—Caden's reaction, "What are you doing out?!" attests to it—but having experienced the death of a father, I do feel comfortable acknowledging and identifying with the murky reaction she's seemingly having to it. The idea most classically stated is to call it "shock," which seems right enough—I feel a bit as if I'm having a stroke while typing this, I'm not sure what's going on; I keep writing the wrong things—but I've also experienced something that I would more comfortably refer to as "shock," and the experience I had in the aftermath of my father's death, and what Claire is seemingly experiencing, don't necessarily align with that experience. Almost immediately, before even the night can end, it cuts, and we're at the funeral for Claire's mother, and Caden is with her, watching, when the priest narrates the mother's life, and Claire softly states to Caden, "I used to be a *baby . . .*" which does, to me, feel strongly connected to the *kind* of emotional reaction I had to the death of my father. It is, in a way, the beginning of our final real birth into existence, the other parent's death being the other half of it—I'm emotional today, and not particularly well, and not, honestly, feeling as if I'm approaching this subject matter correctly, but since we know that Kaufman experiences this, and since Caden experiences this (he more or less just acknowledged, moments prior, that he does not know what he's doing—but was it only moments prior?)—and although Claire has, until now, seemed as though she might be taken a bit less seriously than other figures in the film, a bit like Donald Kaufman in *Adaptation*, it's clear that she is coming into her own, and by extension so is Caden, both literally, because he is enacting his vision and Claire is an essential part of it, and probably metaphorically in either one of two ways, (1) Caden, being a writer and a director, is a reflection of Kaufman the writer/director, and his relationship to his actors is strong, and they are realizing his vision, and thus their experiences are reflections of him, or (2) Aspects of this film continue to, sort of, be ornate components of Caden's imagination, but this isn't something I can continue to believe in a strict sense, because I find readings of texts in this manner to be both annoying and useless, and because the film does seem to want us to read everything that happens in it as essential to *S.N.Y.*, not an invitation to look for subtext, which is probably the most overrated and misunderstood thing especially a filmgoing audience can feel prompted to search for, so we'll let it die now. At the very end of this, Claire is wearing a robe, and brushing her teeth, and looking at what is presumably Caden sitting on her bed, and it's jarring how different this feels from his entanglement with Hazel. With Hazel, the flirtation was up front, and the actual time together once the logical conclusion of said flirtation was reached was simply terrible, and one-sided until both sides wanted to bolt in the opposite direction. With Claire, it's obvious that Caden feels something for her, though it's complicated by the obviousness of this, Caden being her director, and both Caden and Kaufman having an aversion to cliché, but although Claire has occasionally played into the sort of wispy ingenue motif, she's clearly doing so because she takes her acting seriously, as she's almost always immediately dismissive of herself and her perspective, referring to herself as a sort of absent-minded naif, as opposed to someone consciously using her obvious appeal to her male counterparts to achieve something in an aggressive manner. Although her emotional reaction to her mother's death and funeral seems off, she seems very much in control of what she wants, and what she wants, seemingly more than anything, is to do the serious work as an actor she feels compelled to do, which again aligns her entirely with Caden's vision, though at present he's probably at least slightly preoccupied by the fact that this woman wants him around.

Minute 46

It is Caden in the bed, and Claire approaches, and they quickly entangle, and Caden states "I have to fuck you. I have to," and presumably they fuck, and then it cuts—while the priest from Claire's mother's funeral is still narrating her life, now moving into Claire's life, her being bitten by the acting bug, starring in *Oklahoma*, and so on—to Claire and Caden getting married, surrounded by people, and then it cuts again to Caden standing in a line, holding a box addressed to Olive that looks to be exactly the same size as the Pink Nose box, and we can read that he's written himself as *Daddy "Santa"* on the box, so the weird adherence to seemingly several timelines simultaneously asserts the probable meaninglessness of actual time to this narrative, and Caden's emotional relationship to the time he's spent away from Adele and Olive. Caden is now a bigamist. Cut: a man stands at a table in what looks to be the "locker room" of the warehouse where they're beginning their production, and says he'd like to buy a ticket, and Claire is sitting there, playing Hazel, with red hair now or a red wig, and a slightly more homely Sgt. Pepper's-style button-down cardigan, and before they can continue Caden stops them, telling them that they all—Caden included, he says "We"— need to investigate, need to dig into the essence of each being. I do think Proust is important here. I'm also tempted to see aspects of this as a further critique of autobiographical writing that's started in *Adaptation*. This does, though, feel more like Proust, that is, the one kind of autobiographical storytelling that actually and perpetually justifies its own existence. I don't mean Kaufman's autobiography, but that's a natural-enough connection. Caden, as evidenced by the scene being performed, is processing his own direct experience in what he's staging, taking from extremely recent history to construct the beginning of his masterpiece, which, though not obviously Proustian—we never see young Caden, for instance—when actually delved into, and repeated, and repeated, as Caden does, to the point of exhaustion, to the point of taking on other actors to play himself, to the point of becoming a mere janitor in the production of this repetition, does feel Proustian in every right, a moment distilled not in the manner of literature, so that descriptions of the walls of one's childhood room are swollen, and meandering, and lush, but in the manner of film, which requires that repetition, and variation, and repetition, until the thing is wholly gotten right.

Minute 47

There is an inherent tension in any work of even quasi-surrealism that an audience member feels, and what's interesting is the complete opposite might be said to be the experience of the artist creating the work. The tension, I mean, can not only be nonexistent, but the process of embracing a sort of surrealistic mode can feel like the alleviation of tension, the shedding of a false cloak of narrative mandates, the embrace of something somehow realer than if we'd continued to hem ourselves into expectation and rules for the reality of our story. There are more effective and less effective iterations of this, I think, in Kaufman's work. I mean more effective or less effective in terms of the audience side, since I obviously can't speak to Kaufman's perspective; I can only speculate. I would argue that a less effective iteration of it, or an example of a smattering of less effective surrealistic moments, would be in *Being John Malkovich*. Some of this, I'm realizing, is down to the actor, the protagonist of the film. John Cusack is a fine actor, and for much of that film he's fantastic, but there's an energy that he can take on where he seems to be particularly excited about talking quickly and angrily, and summarizing something with a crazed, manic energy that the audience is meant to feel quite impressed by. His quick speech in *High Fidelity*, for instance, as compared with his attempts at sense-making in a film like *1408*. Some of the surrealistic elements, then, like the arrangement of floors in the office, or the logic around entering into John Malkovich's brain, feel sort of hampered by John Cusack's relationship to the same, since he is more or less our anchor to this unconvention. Philip Seymour Hoffman, contrarily, has no such mode. If he's speaking quickly in a movie, we're almost not certain he's going to pull it off. We think he might forget something. His natural mode of being is just that: natural. He's best when he's himself, or when he's not perceptibly *trying*, because he never seems to be thinking of what to do next; he never seems to be thinking of what his lines might be. Claire and Caden are now married, and they have a daughter, Ariel, and after the session working with the actors, which Caden ended going off with the male actor, they're having dinner and Claire is talking about her dissatisfaction with how Caden acted, her anger at being neglected. Although I can imagine an audience member watching this and really loving the fact that Caden is with someone now, and what's more she's an actor, and what's more she's deeply involved in his masterpiece, there's a nice bit of ironic distance kept that keeps all of this from feeling too claustrophobic, too surreal, too "crazy." At one point, Caden is looking at a magazine and sees his daughter, Olive, with rose tattoos lining the sides of her body. She looks to be maybe eleven years old, and given the age of Ariel this is probably an impossibility, and Caden is mildly frazzled, saying "she's tattooed!" he's determined to get to his daughter, to help her. Claire says that his daughter's right here, everything's right here, and in as pitch-perfect a moment of black comedy I've witnessed, Caden quickly, dismissively says "my real daughter," and Claire freaks out. It really doesn't seem like the kind of thing that should feel funny, should feel relieving, considering its tragic heft, and yet it does, and I remember the scattered laughter in the theater when it happened, people sort of puzzling through this question quickly of why it's hitting them and making them laugh, and then simply embracing the experience. Another absolute masterpiece of Kaufman's humor happens here as well: after screaming that she's tattooed, Claire dismisses him, saying "Everyone's tattooed!" and lifts the back of her shirt to reveal a massive, top-to-bottom back-covering tattoo of a red and black devil figure, to which Caden responds "I've never seen that before!" His freakout is arrived at in this natural way, and even then never approaches the exquisite "Pig fuck!" freakout of *The Master*. In a weird way, it feels like *The Honeymooners*, or *Married With Children*, or what makes it so funny is that we're given more or less the *setup* of sitcoms like that, and almost nothing within *S.N.Y.* abides by the logic of such a setup. In much the same way that the film runs counter to genius-artist narratives we've been given since forever, its willingness to offer expectation and then defy them in quieter, simpler ways than we might get in an angry, spiteful parody lets the laughter feel as natural as Hoffman.

Minute 48

To write this I've put on John Cage's "Sonata V (from Sonatas and Interludes)—Inara Ferreira, prepared piano," on YouTube, and as I watch and write I can see there have been screws inserted between the strings of the piano. I wanted to listen to something by John Cage because I could feel myself going a bit insane fixating on the film at the present moment. This is a question of method. On the one hand, *S.N.Y.* is a film that has not been analyzed in this way, and thus it is exciting to do it at all, and I'll continue. On the other, occasionally the movement will take on an energy—most often, I've found, when the film is focusing on the absence of Adele and Olive from Caden's life— that feels a lot like living those experiences, that is, torpidity, depression in the medical sense, disinterest, sorrow, misery, ambient pain. These are difficult states to write about in life, and these are difficult states to write about in narratives that render them. A song, then, some little lens through which to look, a sort of sidebar to the feeling that nevertheless feels apt to what I'm trying to say about what I'm seeing, seemed to make sense. I find, though, that the song is only one minute and thirty-nine seconds long, which is unfortunate. It almost instantly goes to a video of Glenn Gould, which isn't imperfect to the task, but I like the idea of staying with it. Perhaps, I think, I can find a replayable version of it. I log into Spotify which I got again for a deal for three months, which I don't feel great about honestly given the slew of what seems like justifiable criticism of their trajectory, but the deal was decent. I put it on and it's stranger than the video version. It's performed by Hiroshi Yokoyama. It could be the score for this particular scene in the film, which shows Caden on a plane, flying from America to Germany, presumably, to visit Olive and to deal with the fact of her tattoo. On the plane he's reading his therapist's book, which commentates on his reality, and which reveals that she's on the plane next to him, and they then speak, and she stands up, walking seductively to him and lifting the bottom of her skirt up over her thigh and pressing it against him. He's confused. We're confused. It's working, however, this shift in energy. It's a sort of microcosmic transference experience, since we haven't gone through that—I don't think, perhaps we have—with this therapist in this film just yet. It also feels like the kind of thing that's probably more suggestive of Caden's consciousness than anything else, though I don't wish to suggest it isn't actually happening in the context of S.N.Y. I think, in tangible and intangible ways, Caden's consciousness *is* S.N.Y., as the moods of the music seem to reflect, and as his fixations and obsessions and the lapses in time inherent to growing older seem to offer us. It is a weird moment, though no less warm for it. We are, or I am, susceptible to this kind of thing, a brief fixation. When I was a kid in therapy, really young, seven years old or so, my immediate reaction was always to fantasize about such things with the therapist. They are always women, which happened to align with my sense of my proclivity, sure. I don't think, either, that I was always looking for an exact sexual act in this fantasizing. I was seven, after all. I didn't have all the pieces yet. I think that I perceive warmth in this otherwise probably perceptibly or sensorily cold scene—it takes place on an airplane, after all, when a man is panickedly trying to reclaim his daughter or hug her or something—because, when I was a kid, I only really thought of it along those lines, as a matter of warmth, and the potential warmth of the therapist, which Caden is seemingly also needing at the moment. She sits down, and he goes back to reading her book, which quickly recounts what has just transpired between them, and then states simply "This book is over."

Minute 49

Caden is aging. I'm not certain if those around him we've seen before are aging too, but for Caden I'm certain of it. The years are being unkind to him. That sounds like an insane sentence. I don't mean it in the sort of way it initially reads. It initially reads like someone who's not a native speaker of English wrote it. I don't mean that offensively. I just mean it precisely. What I mean is that the years, as they're persisting, persist in being unkind to Caden. Poor Caden. He wanders the graffitied streets of Berlin, or Germany anyway, and he looks entirely uncomfortable. This is something I've neglected to pay attention to every time I've watched this film over again. I've neglected to think of *comfort*. Is Caden *comfortable*? Does Caden seek comfort? Is comfort a desirable thing for the character-composite of Caden? To say it like this feels pejorative. It feels as though I'm talking down to him. He looks uncomfortable in the manner of a father on vacation. Uncomfortable in the manner of a father, who works as a professor somewhere just beneath prestigious, but perhaps was once prestigious, and thus is certain enough in his knowledge of this one particular subject, and certain too

of his genius, or potential for genius, and thus has let the rest
of himself languish. Aside from certain aspects I feel as though
I'm describing myself. The "genius" aspects, if you must know.
They aren't things I wish to think about, at least not publicly.
He looks uncomfortable as he wanders into the small gallery
where the walls are littered with the paintings of Adele, who
now goes by Adele Lack. I say "littered with" but this is really
foolish to say. Perhaps I'm aping the language of Maria, her
faux-accent. I'm not sure. Littered with is foolish because her
paintings are willfully tiny, and must be looked at with lenses.
They are separated, but even then they're so tiny that to say
"littered with" is nonsense. What I mean to say is that it is a
gallery primarily displaying Adele Lack's works, and Caden
asks after her. The gallerist instantly says she couldn't possibly
reveal her whereabouts. Caden says he's her husband. The
gallerist says that's impossible, her husbands are "Gunther und
Heinz." We cut then to the device of Olive's diary, which has
taken on its magical characteristic of updating itself for Caden
as he and Olive move throughout their lives, and which is fine,
perfectly fine. When Maria finally approaches Caden, we no
longer care very much about his comfort or his discomfort,
because again Kaufman's acumen with comedy is so perfectly
placed and so readied it's like nothing else. Maria lovingly,
flowingly gives her "Hallo," and Caden's response is perfect, a
beauty, a masterpiece: "*You're* here?!"

Minute 50

It would seem impossible for Caden not to snap, to absolutely
lose it at some point over the course of this narrative, his
life. Maria's accent is now French, as she's the nanny, and
she's even wearing, underneath a T-shirt, with jeans—it's a
very metropolitan mom look—a sort of billowy white and
black blouse suggesting the garb of a French maid, possibly
an inversion of the usual affair trope we might expect were

Caden the usual genius-artist-husband-protagonist. This also feels like a nice little jab at the people who semester in the UK and return to America calling chips "crisps." Caden becomes incensed, consumed with rage at his predicament, at what they're doing to his daughter. "They had her tattooed!" he screams at Maria. "I did that," Maria responds, claiming Olive is her muse. "She's a four-year-old! A fucking four-year-old!" We find out she's actually closer to eleven. This is simply too much to take. For any father probably it's too much to take. Caden has existed in a kind of ambivalent ownership of his existence until now, commenting on it and effecting certain changes, but largely letting it wash over him. Now he cannot take it, it's just too much. He screams and grabs Maria violently, wrestling her to the ground in a still slightly pathetic manner, clearly not wanting to beat the life out of her or strangle her, clearly even regretting what he'd done but following his impulse, his emotions. The tide turns instantly, and Maria is on top of Caden's back, and out of there before anything further can happen.

Minute 51

He's seemingly chasing Maria but turns into an empty sort of alley, though it's not a road exactly so much as the spot where a building tosses out its trash. I think *Beau Is Afraid* and *S.N.Y.* are brothers, which makes me wonder about finding elements of *S.N.Y.* in Jacques Tati. In this space, he finds the Pink Nose box, discarded among the surrounding refuse. Really interestingly here Caden takes out a bottle of "Tear Substitute," and squirts it into both of his eyes before walking to the box and having a good cry. There are moments throughout the film that overtly comment on the made-up nature of its reality, and the inherent weirdness that these characters' work as theater professionals and artists exerts on this reality, but few are as overt as this. The immediate association here for me is the scene in the diner where Caden's forcing himself to swallow. That's not any commentary on theater, or artifice, of course, but the sort of pathetic nature of this whole ordeal feels closer to what's happening on screen than some cheap metacommentary on fictive cinema. Caden sits there, performatively crying, but really the performance is Hoffman's performance, and Hoffman is, to take the film at its word, Caden, and thus his fake crying is real, in the sense that he's being up front about his inability to cry, though no less determined to cry at this very tragic instance in his existence. I'm not trying to be as circuitous as I'm coming across. I only mean to say that it is possible for blatant artifice to exist alongside a beautiful, expressive art, and for nothing to be sacrificed in pulling back the curtain a bit. Here Tati makes more and more sense, and *Playtime* in particular—the use of props throughout that pull us out of scenarios long enough to chuckle, or quickly think, before we're pulled right back into the world being enacted—and given the eventual function of Caden's warehouse the fixation on a building as a locus for compelling engagement with modernity feels right. Where Kaufman differs, I think, is in his brand of sorrow, that is, I think, again, it's possible to read Caden's actions in this moment as earnest, as "real," and as indicative of the pain he's incapable of wholly accessing. I remember my first time watching this film. I loved it and I didn't love it. I found its comedy deeply warm, human, and its sorrow connective, but I struggled because it didn't smack of the sharp iterations of sorrow, of anxiety, I'd only really felt back then. Now, being older, having experienced long stretches of anhedonia, sorrow, anxiety, indifference, ambivalence, I see in Caden an illustration of the twenty-first century's opening archetype. It bugged me, I remember, that he *wasn't* more extreme, much in the way that Hoffman's Lancaster Dodd character in P. T. Anderson's *The Master* doesn't feel, at first glance, remotely as compelling as Joaquin Phoenix's Freddie Quell. There's almost an annoyance I'd felt, like rubbing my fingertips over Styrofoam, and it kept me from fully experiencing the films. Life, though, equalizes all of us, and the passing of Hoffman, and the slow realization that he's certainly my favorite actor; these things converged and now these moments stir me, move me in a way that feels like lived experience, and almost makes me weep. "Death comes faster than you think."

Minute 52

The making of art is constantly being pulled in two directions. What I mean to say is that an artist, making any artwork, is constantly being yanked by two energies. One toward the future, toward futurity, potential, possibility, *openness*. The other toward tradition, reference, citation, history. I often find myself thinking during performances I've witnessed, or recordings of performances, about the lives of the people performing, and about bad days that I've had, and days in which I had to do something whether my day was bad or not, especially when what was making them bad had nothing to do with what I had to do. Working an average job, say, when you're in a relationship, and you're in one of those fights that simply refuses to end, and both of you are completely worn down, and you might briefly surface into a reasonable space, wherein you both want to be OK, and maybe you even briefly become intimate, before returning swiftly back to total acrimony. I recently took my children to see a local performance of *Fiddler on the Roof*. I don't know if I'd ever seen it live. My father loved it, so I remembered certain songs and the like. I felt excited to take my children to this, and they enjoyed the experience, and I tried to extend it into conversations outside of the event. When we were sitting there, though, with the old man playing Tevye, and the teenagers playing the daughters or the locals, I found myself wondering if any of them were fighting with their significant others, and whether all they wanted to do was return to them, or even just to their phone, which they were certain would be filled up with messages, and which, during those brutal fights, almost never is. Caden is now directing, and they are building inside of the warehouse, and we follow him as he moves along the spaces of his construction. We see a reimagining of an earlier scene in Caden's life with a doctor. We see a therapy appointment that's probably a rendering of Caden's from earlier. We see Caden's new daughter, and Claire, who is now the polar opposite of Adele. She's outwardly bitter at Caden, furious that he's left them to "find himself," but still a part of the performance, and thus it's not clear what of this is simply a part of his construction or a necessary way to accommodate his actual life, and of course it's growing and will continue to grow more and more impossible to differentiate between these states. Caden, then, is able to find some balance in the physical ritual of constructing this artifice, this meaning, this performance, because of its reaching toward tradition, toward history, toward the world of art and its role in his life, and what's doubly compelling is he's seemingly managed to account for the hand reaching in the other direction, toward futurity, and chaos, and the unknown, and openness, by letting it all into the piece.

Minute 53

Back to the doctor's office, that's even bleaker, more dimly lit and flickering, the hospital bed seemingly plopped in the middle of the room at random, everything dark. This time Caden's leg is twitching rampantly, and it feels, again, made-up. He doesn't really let on, though, Caden, he cuts right to the chase and asks the doctor if he can tell him if he's dying. The doctor, of course, doesn't bite, and basically only says "No" to every question asked. This is the summary of their interaction, but what we get from it is a firmer sense that Caden is beginning to spiral. Afterwards, he's walking down the street and runs into Hazel, and though it isn't clear precisely where they are, it's clear that he hadn't expected to see her in this particular place—I'd say that *S.N.Y.* is light on "place," that its locations rarely feel super significant, *excepting* of course when they're inside the warehouse—and though they'd seen each other previously, it's also apparent that at that point Hazel wasn't ready to engage with Caden like this, because there's a warmth and energy to both of them now that wasn't apparent before.

Minute 54

They are in New York. Caden is experiencing the highly relatable and often avoidable sorrow of connecting too excitedly with persons from one's past. It's a visceral, heaping emotion that hits him, and hits us, standing there holding onto the metal bar of a fence in a nice New York neighborhood talking to this woman. Just moments ago, it seemed, they were in bed together, unable to have sex. Or rather, Caden was unable, Hazel was rejected and angry. Now she's with Derek, and they have five children. She looks well and happy. Caden, again, just looks uncomfortable. His hair is graying and receding. His shirt is an ill-fitting plaid-patterned white button-up that looks like the sort of thing a middle school science teacher who hates his life would wear. He's seemingly stopping himself from breaking down into tears, and the weight of this emotion is communicated so effectively it's almost as if it's magic. It came out of nowhere, really. And the illogical nature of time in this film would seemingly preclude our getting too invested in any one moment's weight all that much, but here we are. Before he was foibling, he was a bumbling doofus, and it was wonderful. Now he is honest and separated from Claire and his second daughter, and it's cutting to watch. This entire transformation has happened jarringly quick, and the mood of it is not an offensive sadness, not the kind of thing we typically resent or shun or run from. It's been built to in an honest manner. There has been no attempt to deceive us to get here. We are feeling what Caden is feeling.

Minute 55

They hug, and part, but immediately Caden follows Hazel, observing her and her family on a nice hotel patio deck overlooking the city, laughing together and feeling joyous. This sends Caden spiraling, so he slowly walks over to the edge of the balcony, surely out of sight of Hazel and her family, and starts to awkwardly climb over it to jump, to commit suicide. Almost instantly, a man nearby grabs him and prevents him from doing it, but Caden screams for him to let him go, which of course has no effect on the man, who brings him back to the hotel patio deck in sorrow, and the building wave of music that's slowly repeated since seeing Hazel reaches its crescendo, and our feeling what Caden's feeling prior to this makes all of it now feel so defeated. We are defeated. Caden is defeated. We have failed even to commit suicide, if that is in fact what we truly wanted. It's unclear. Perhaps Caden saw the man nearby. We can't be sure. We know that he was making every awkward effort to climb over, and it didn't look to be the kind of balcony railing where he might've stood there a while until the fire department came. Weirdly, the setup of the balcony reminded me of Harold Lloyd films. These close-together skyscraper walls and dramatically set arrangement surrounded by people. This is almost certainly projection. And now Olive is growing up, and Caden is reading her diary, which is now accented like Maria, wherein she's discussing Caden's failures as a father, his drinking, his body odor, his rotting teeth; and Maria's presence as a father counterbalancing this. It's bleak, but it's the kind of thing that might take out the weight of a failed suicide attempt, the sheer absurd energy of it.

Minute 56

Caden moves from misery to misery, from event to event, and though it's a reduction to say it's all on this downward trajectory, his proximity to still newer lows has begun to feel almost warm, a comfort, something to be sought. After reading Olive's diary he can't take it, so he goes to Claire's door, knocking until she answers, telling her he wants to come back, again misremembering his daughter with Claire, whose name is Ariel. I am slightly averse to the easter egg. I don't like a reference unless it's a natural thing, and in this case I don't know that I'd call it one—discussions of Proust are natural, in a film about aging, recurrence, dying; readings and commentaries on Rilke are natural in turn—but in such a film it's tough to hear the name "Ariel" and not think of Sylvia Plath.

> Stasis in darkness.
> Then the substanceless blue
> Pour of tor and distances.
> God's lioness,
> How one we grow,
> Pivot of heels and knees!—The furrow
> Splits and passes, sister to
> The brown arc
> Of the neck I cannot catch,[9]

This is not a thing that's said, but unless a film is reaching *Histoire(s) du Cinema* levels of intercutting and quotation one of the devices at hand at present is my own association. And like Proust and Kafka and Rilke it mightn't even need to be the poem itself, it could simply be that one connection—and of course the weirder question underneath it is what I'm to make of his true paternal yearning for a child simply named "Olive," but such is life. I think, too, that this is what you get when you make a film that does not aspire to be slick, or smarter than anyone else, or God forbid a work of "genius." Tom Noonan's character returns, but I'm quite convinced he's been scattered throughout the thing thus far and I just haven't paid close enough attention in the however-many screenings there've been. This time it's while Claire and Caden are in bed together, and Caden looks over and briefly sees this man, sitting with Ariel in his lap, and looks away and then he's gone. Then it seems as if he calls Caden on the phone—at least the voice sounds like it to me—and we see who's presumably Noonan's character in shadow outside their bedroom window. Caden acknowledges that the phone call informed him that his father has died. When Claire and Caden get together this happens, in mirror. A phrase such as that: "Stasis in darkness/Then the substanceless blue/Pour of tor and distances," is just the kind of thing you want to be thinking about at such a time. Having experienced the phone call informing me of the death of my own father, I feel slightly alien from Caden's experience. He's older, and facing an existence thick with sorrow and uncertainty, so in this respect I'm quite lucky. That sense, however, of wanting to simply lay one's head down on the pillow, not say much of anything at all, to simply rest and think about this man with whom you have, as a son and a father yourself and an artist whose father is not those things—we can infer, I think, safely enough—such difficult thoughts, such impossible feelings.

Minute 57

Hoffman's performance of Caden is not the kind I think of in terms of monologuing. There are not "halftime speeches" in *S.N.Y.* They wouldn't fit. And probably Kaufman's great asset is his ability to exact similar moments from dialogue, from moments like Donald and Charlie Kaufman speaking at the end of *Adaptation*—"I just got shot! Isn't that fucked up?!"—or his interactions with the fictional Brian McKee in the same, as opposed to your big *What-have-I-done-with-my-life* orations we might get from Paul Thomas Anderson & co. Caden monologues, then, but interactively, telling Claire "They said . . ." statements that continue into their bleakness, darker and darker until a small stitch of relief comes. We hear that his father had given the saddest and longest deathbed

speech they'd ever heard, and it's somewhere in here that a
relief comes, not quite in laughter, but in this commitment
nevertheless to the bit of this ordeal, which is tragic, yes, but it's
so extremely tragic as to approach Kafka, and though reading
"The Metamorphosis" can feel like a tragic experience for
modern readers, it's important to note that Kafka's neighbors
at the time had to complain because he wouldn't stop howling
with laughter and stomping his feet at what he wrote. Caden's
father, somehow, had grown so small in dying that his coffin
is child-size, and had to be filled with cotton balls to avoid his
"rattling around."

Minute 58

Caden sits on the couch after his father's funeral being
consoled, then tells Claire he needs to use the bathroom,
where he tries to call Hazel. There's a weird self-sabotage here,
a strain of which probably runs through every minute of this
film, where he's only drawn to recent intimate weirdnesses
instead of whatever's right in front of him. Adele *could* be the
exception, but we have the sense that their affairs were mutual.
He can't reach her, so later that night he sits outside her house,
where she lives with Derek and five children, and which is still
on fire, to ask her simply to tell him what to do. In a way it
feels very teenage, but as with weddings there does seem to be
an aspect of funerals that generates a kind of desperation in
certain people, of whom Caden is certainly a member. It's sad,
though, to see this disparity constantly between what could
be, and what the action of the individual realizes. This is the
problem of the Will, in Schopenhauerian terms. Too much
willing, to simplify it, could be pointed to as the genesis of just
about every problem. Art, for Schopenhauer, can be an escape
from this, but the real world, and lived experience, has plucked
Caden from that context, and thus his willing, his desiring,
renders the whole thing uglier.

Minute 59

You truly can never return when it comes to this kind of intimacy. Probably there are historical exceptions—Harry Crews remarried his wife, I think, but I believe they got divorced again thereafter—but this compulsion is to be resisted at all costs. When vulnerable, it seems, a person wishes to go back to the way things were, and what better way to realize this vision than to mix with an actual person that represents this; and yet, they don't, not really. They represent—again, Schopenhauer—a fiction in Caden's head, a dream of what was, blurred by rose color, and thus he can sit in the car with Hazel and act as if they're going to get back together, and she can sit there knowing this isn't going to happen, and he can sit there convinced it's the one true solution to his plight; and we can watch the both of them spinning around it, Caden not wanting to acknowledge something he's feeling, Hazel wanting simply to go back inside the house, to the new life she's built because she had to—and even this feels extreme, Caden wasn't ever going to be her husband, the father of her children; it never seemed that way for them. It's a form of tragedy that often goes unexplored, the lagging ships passing, the one having reached some milder, satisfactory version, the other having circled and realized there's nothing for them, and so clinging to this false memory, circling then by shore and screaming that this is what's finally right. It's bleak, but it's a rarity in dramatic work, and beautiful.

Minute 60

The music in this film, though not the kind of music I would probably choose were I making similar material, nor the kind of thing I often like to listen to, is simply perfect and simply beautiful—though this is probably mainly in the context of the film itself, because it's not the kind of thing I find myself listening to when I'm not watching it. Caden's movement through the world is accompanied by simple piano, rising and falling, after reading Olive's diary and hearing of her growing into a woman, and then, we infer from the writings on the posters on the street surrounding him, Caden seemingly returns to Berlin to find her. His hair is receding more significantly now. His sorrow has transformed into a natural state, which is somehow acceptable, like when we've endured some hellish day and we simply become resigned to it. Caden seems to have accepted it, is no longer fighting it so aggressively. He sees a poster indicating where to find Olive, connected with her prior tattooing, and enters a sleazy hallway with red cinderblock walls, where a line of men look back at him or straight ahead. We've entered a shameful place, we can feel, and for Caden it simply brings sorrow. He is low.

Minute 61

There's a moment of real misery when it becomes clear that he's not waiting in the hallway, sitting against the bricks, but in the room where Olive is. She's working. She's naked, with rose tattoos up and down the arms and sides of her body. She's blowing bubbles, moving around seductively. For a moment, Caden simply looks at her, and then starts to knock against the glass separating them, through which, of course, Olive sees nothing; or if she can see, she doesn't see Caden, or doesn't want to, or she's on drugs, or she's looked or given in to people doing crazy things at the window previously and she's not making that mistake again. There's a doubly weird moment when Caden's screaming "Olive! It's Daddy!" and we have to think of prior customers saying similar things under extremely different circumstances. Again, as before, Olive is what sets him off, what makes him lose it, and he starts hitting the glass more aggressively. Too aggressively, as security comes in and begins escorting him out, to which Caden screams "it's my *daughter*!"

to no avail. We briefly imagine other fathers having gone through precisely this same moment before. As with previous extremes, this prompts Caden to return to work. We first see Claire, seated, with presumably Caden walking back and forth in front of her, and hear Caden speaking. Claire has aged, her hair is different, the sense of youthful energy is basically gone. She looks dignified, though, in a white button-up shirt with a sort of artist's scarf around her neck. She doesn't seem happy to be there, but there's a nice sense nevertheless that she either wants or needs to be there, for her sense of her work. It looks as though the warehouse might've had a fire, or like it never got refurbished where they are. Caden states, with real energy now: "I won't settle for anything less than the brutal truth."

Minute 62

"Brutal. Brutal." This moment perfectly articulates the necessity of art for the artist, regardless of audience—and in this scene we get the fact that the warehouse piece has been worked over for seventeen years, and a cast member wonders whether they'll ever be getting an audience at all—because amid all the horrible things Caden endures up until this scene, the solace that he's able to find in the work he's doing doesn't feel out of line with those actual experiences. This is not to say that every artist is best served by doing this very thing, but there is a real genius in recognizing the aspects of one's existence that might best be transformed into one's work. This can prove thorny, especially in the lives of figures like Burroughs or Bukowski, where the life serving the work can become a snake eating its own tail and sustaining itself on the myths surrounding the artist—of course in the former's case the work did continue to push into ever more interesting places, where the latter wound up really boring. For Caden, though, there's little romanticizing or self-mythologizing. We get it a tiny bit when he states "my lonely, *fucked-up*, existence," with probably a little too much swagger than the moment calls for, but we're free to recognize it either as a flaw in Philip Seymour Hoffman's performance, or an actual reflection of the perspective of Caden, a progressively more monomaniacal theater director creating a piece over seventeen years in a massive, impossible warehouse after losing everything and wanting somehow to hold onto what matters most through his work, that is, a bit of swagger can feel icky, and it's OK.

Minute 63

Synecdoche, New York directed by Charlie Kaufman © Sony Pictures Classics 2008. All rights reserved.

"Nothing matters anymore." "Your wife just had a miscarriage." "You keep biting your tongue." "You were raped last night." "You lost your job today."

Caden sits at a table that's really multiple tables pushed together so that he can write out these notes to his performers and set them out in front of himself. They look like the notebook pages torn from a spiral journalist's notebook. It's interesting to think of what's on the rest of them. Something like "Nothing matters anymore" feels kind of weightless and difficult for an actor to make sense of, but the more we see, the more we realize how receiving more than one of them could really stir something within us. There's also a parallel that was drawn between this and *Playtime*, the moment when we're looking over the top of Hulot as he looks down upon the workers in their cubicles. This is also probably the most circulated still from the film. Since the very first time I read the screenplay for Bergman's *Persona*, it's the first time I can remember feeling really awed by the kind of energy that can be put into this kind of work. I've never loved Bergman, but *Persona* always really affected me, and when I found out it was possible to buy the screenplay in book form, I had to, and when I did, it was comprised of strange, elliptical, compressed material like this, which I really enjoyed reading more than I've enjoyed watching the majority of Bergman's other films. The scene cuts before we can see much else, to Hazel, sitting on a park bench, crying mildly and talking into the phone about how she's been fired. She's talking to Caden. She gave everyone conjunctivitis, as it turns out. The Christian private school she and Derek send their kids to is costly, and she needs something, and there's a weird energy here that sometimes happens either in narratives or in life where someone is able to reject someone after they've been rejected (Hazel), but time inevitably circles back around, and Caden is then sort of sought after by the person who'd rejected him after he'd rejected her. I only say this because there's this weird divulgence, "You know I don't believe in that shit," about the Christian school, how it's Derek's thing, which feels slightly sneaky, a shared little secret of her dissatisfaction. The music is this wonderful building campus film cello. Caden's in his office with another assistant. He's working. Things feel righted.

Minute 64

Tom Noonan is Sammy Barnathan, and when he's interviewed as the performer to shadow Caden he's seemingly listening to

the score for the film in the scenes preceding. He tells Caden
that he's been following him for twenty years, and to hire him,
"so you'll see who you truly are," and there's something so
calming yet deeply disconcerting in Tom Noonan's presence.
I suppose I should have said "Sammy Barnathan" just then,
but I do think Noonan is that kind of performer, as he seems
to embody this weird mixture in other roles, and I also think
it's how there manages to be a certain level of heart injected
into this dynamic. You see, if "transgressive" art is to have any
relevance or meaning anymore, it's largely in this capacity,
not in shockjockism or dealing solely with crime; though
Barnathan's stalking is technically criminal, it's not remotely
presented in that manner. What I mean is there's a clear
line that might be said to be crossed in this interaction, this
dynamic, but because of what's been laid before it the line
doesn't even seem to exist. Barnathan tells Caden he's not an
actor, and Caden quickly responds "Good," as though he's sick
of actors, and any taboos that have been broken or abutted
against in Barnathan's stalking feel elided by the new spaces of
logic opened up by the energy of the rest of the film. Further,
that warmth I mentioned, where Barnathan felt driven to
follow Caden, and sort of hovers around him for the rest of
the film, taking him over bodily, metaphorically speaking; if
we had this dynamic introduced in something more clearly
lined up with our contemporary existence's values, we'd feel
put off, bothered by it—and certainly there are viewers who
still do, even after everything they've already seen in *S.N.Y.*—
but for those of us who've let the unique logic of this world
wash over us, a new space for human being, for empathy, for
identification, can be opened up.

Minute 65

Barnathan then asserts, in Caden's stead, that they don't need
to see anybody else, that Barnathan has him figured out. He

continues into a monologue from Caden's perspective about wanting to fuck Hazel, who's sitting next to Caden and watching Barnathan, and wanting "to merge into a chimera, a mythical beast with penis and vagina eternally-fused," and it's weird, because on the one hand I don't think he sounds particularly close to Caden, not in manner of speech nor in the brazen way he's operating—it appears as if he's been convincing himself of what he should do here, and he's decided finally just to give himself over to it—but there's also something charming about *this* particular take on Caden being the thing that convinces Caden, and though the mostly mumbling, very occasionally angry or passionate version of Caden is the version we largely get in *S.N.Y.*, it's not completely impossible that what he's presenting back to Caden is inaccurate. What's really interesting, actually, is to think that Barnathan somehow anticipates all of this, and that what he's presenting back to Caden is a version of Caden that Caden either sees himself as or aspires to be, which seems entirely reasonable.

Minute 66

Quite quickly we understand the appeal of Barnathan for Caden, but there's a nice moment when he's told that he got the part, and Caden sits there, and that recurring piano theme begins to play, and Caden has one of those realizations you sometimes have in life, when everything has not even remotely played out how you thought it would, and maybe things even feel kind of crazy in comparison, like you couldn't have anticipated them to even want them if you'd tried, but still you've managed to put together your little version of heaven with these wonderful freaks, who are—especially here, aspirationally so, anyway—just like you. Then Caden is standing in the bathroom, looking down at his stool, and freakishly tall Tom Noonan's Barnathan is standing over the divider, watching him, observing the stool. They go out to wash hands, Barnathan jotting observations of Caden in a small notebook, and says "I've never seen your shit gray," and Caden replies "It's new." This is another thing that feels impossible in most other fictive narrative contexts: A character finding out that a grown man has been watching him enough, and has presumably somehow been monitoring the colors of his stools frequently enough to make such a comment. In most any context it would be jarring, but because of the emotional beating both Caden and the audience have sort of suffered by proxy in bearing witness to it, it's become sweet, as though Barnathan were Caden's guardian angel. Caden takes out a massive handful of pills and supplements, and swallows them with a small sip from a bottle of water. Barnathan pats him on the shoulder, saying "Good boy," and again, it seems to reach a new level of emotion, becomes more touching, because of this totally strange but earnest context in which we've found it. Then Caden is shown leaving the place with Claire and Ariel, and we hear militaristic gunshots in the distance, and someone standing outside asks when it's going to be open. Initially it seems exciting because there seems already to be an audience for the work, but then he explains how dangerous it is out there, at which point the gunshots continue. Caden says "when it's ready," and continues walking. It seems the world, in the unknowable span of time since this story began, has gone to hell. It seems, too, that Caden's work has taken on a curious metaphorical dimension for us, where the work can now be seen as something potentially lifesaving for people in this hellish context. It feels a bit unlike Kaufman to set this kind of thing up, so it's not something I'm particularly attached to—probably the hellish world is closer to a reflection of the weird temporal stuff happening—but the level of "commentary" someone like Tati is comfortable with in *Playtime* seems perfectly fine in this context (there's way more of the Tati commentary stuff in Aster's *Beau Is Afraid*, though there it seems played mainly for humor)—and, of course, I reserve the right to hold out for the very likely possibility that Kaufman hadn't even seen *Playtime* when *S.N.Y.* was made, because that kind of thing seems to happen all the time. Either way, seeing the moment of Caden leaving the work for the day is deeply grounding, like seeing anyone at the end of their working day, picking up their kids or running errands. Until now the scenes within the warehouse felt out of time, or as if they were constantly happening, or happening at the end of whatever else in the film happens, so it's nice to see him in the evening, even if it's to understand that the world he's walking out into is apocalyptic.

Minute 67

Here we get Caden's first idea for a title for the Work: *Simulacrum*. Caden is walking with Claire, Ariel, and Sammy, back home, after the interaction outside of the warehouse. Claire responds that she doesn't even know what it means, so we quickly get another of Caden's title ideas: *The Flawed Light of Love and Grief*, and there's an important aspect of *S.N.Y.*, and probably titles in general, that this device brings up. We get further title ideas throughout the development of the work. There have also been countless conversations, with Kaufman, without Kaufman, about why this particular film is called what it's called. Much in the way of a film like *Reservoir Dogs*, where the title is memorable, seemingly *adjacent* to its subject matter (somehow), and cryptic enough, people find themselves speculating endlessly about its possible meanings. Kaufman acknowledged in an interview with *Vulture* that he'd put together a set of possible titles, *Synecdoche, New York* being the one that he was fondest of, and thus it stayed. This acknowledgment, though, commingled with the device of Caden repeating title ideas in the film, drives home a weird commitment I have to this notion that titles are simultaneously totally unimportant and absolutely essential. What I mean by this is: If it gets you into the experience, it's absolutely essential. If it, however, alienated you, kept you out, made you feel like you didn't "get it," or something, then it's completely unimportant. I know such a thing isn't possible, but part of me likes the idea of *S.N.Y.* having a revolving title or something, including the titles Caden presents for the Work. Then Ariel asks if she can have some money if she doesn't play with her pee-pee. Then we see Caden and Sammy Barnathan sitting on the back balcony of the apartment Claire and Caden share, and a nice strain of humor is introduced back into everything, with Barnathan making small adjustments to his person as he observes Caden, doing his best to immerse himself wholly in this role. They discuss Barnathan moving in with Claire, and she's hesitant, but Sammy chimes in just right, praising her acting ability, referencing a play he had seen her in that past summer, and you can't shake this wonderful feeling that they've gotten the band back together.

Minute 68

Caden and Barnathan quickly arrive at a back-and-forth that's connective (for us) and hilarious. Claire's excited about her performance, playing herself now with an actor playing Caden, and tells them at the window that she'll start thinking about herself (i.e., how to perform herself). Barnathan quickly jokes, once she's out of earshot, "Start?" and he and Caden laugh heartily. We then hear and see Claire pacing back and forth in the living room repeating "Claire Keen" in different vocal registers. Barnathan—I realize it's more natural to refer to him as Sammy, since he's often referred to that way in the film, but for me at present it's feeling more natural to refer to him as Barnathan, so I do apologize—then asks magnanimously, "Why did we leave Adele, Caden?" To which Caden replies, "She left us, you know that better than anybody. Except me." Barnathan then goes into a lament, calling her the greatest living artist, and mourning this loss. "Sweet pussy, too," he adds, and Caden wonders how he could know that. "Oh, I read it," and they both chuckle. In his referencing Adele as the greatest living artist, it seems as though he's egging Caden on, or at least that seems to be the effect, as Caden gives him a look when he says that nobody else "stares truth in the face like she does," and it kind of feels like the moment when Adele pushes Caden much earlier in the film, reacting to his iteration of *Death of a Salesman*, challenging him to do something with his art that's more ambitious. Barnathan's demeanor, though, is that curious, chameleon-like perspective of the kind of person who likes to see their friends fighting, and will find little ways of peppering conversation as if he's simply interested, then suddenly relish when they come to blows over whatever he'd introduced. I won't testify in court to that effect, but given the predicament the two of these characters are presently in, it hardly feels like I'm stretching the realms of possibility to think he might like egging Caden on, especially if he's motivated by deepening and enhancing the work.

Minute 69

We see Caden and Barnathan's view then, of the city, and there's a massive zeppelin flying around, apparently governmental surveillance spotlighting different parts of the city, and Barnathan's encouraging Caden to see Adele. He tells him she's got a sublet in the city, and that they're doing a retrospective of her work, and that he wants to follow him to "see how you lose even more of himself . . . Research." Any inkling already apparent from Barnathan's strange position is solidified, as it now feels as though he's simply treating Caden sadistically. Caden, ever the masochist—sort of, though he's sort of in control of everything in the sense that he seems to ambiently know that fundamentally he is responsible for his lot, but he's just unwilling to wholly exist within that knowledge—immediately goes to the exhibit of Adele's work, and everyone's walking around with their magnifying rigs they'd had at the exhibit in Germany, like I'd imagine jeweler's wear. He walks about the room, looking at images mostly of Maria, often in the nude, not expressing much but simply observing, taking in the experience, which, in Barnathan's slight defense, Caden seems entirely caught up in. I don't know what to make of the strange state of the city. Is it simply supposed to be temporal? Is it simply some indicator that the world is now quite different, that X number of years have passed, and Caden is quite old? The depiction of time in *S.N.Y.* almost makes it feel as though it's depicting an impossibly distant future, showing the direction in which the world is heading; but there isn't enough explored to that effect to really support this. I don't know that it matters too heavily, but it's something pulling at my consciousness when I look at Caden staring at the artworks. I wondered, too, about the fame of Adele, who paints fairly ornate, expressive pictures of bodies in absolutely tiny frames, in expressive detail rather than immense detail, where the flesh is reddened and human. It isn't that she can simply paint things so small. That doesn't seem like enough to warrant the level of success she's achieved, though perhaps this success is largely informed by *S.N.Y.* operating from Caden's perspective. The art of it, I guess, if the craft of it could be said to be the magnifying devices Adele and the viewer use, and the brushes, seems to be *what* she's made so tiny—nearly microscopic—these highly vulnerable images of lovers, often naked, hiding, that open up like a secret world one might almost possess in a locket.

Minute 70

He leaves and wanders the street, then apparently deciding to find the sublet Barnathan mentioned, and we get a nice *Curb Your Enthusiasm*-meets-*Charlie Brown* moment where depressed, depressive Caden mopes into her elevator, and an old woman rushes to it asking him to hold the door; Caden briefly considers it, even making as though he's going to press the button, but doesn't commit, except she's going to his same floor, it turns out, and shouts after him in the long, dark hallway that he didn't hold the elevator for her. He lies, and she calls him on it. The setup of the city in closeup, and the setup of these building interiors, much like the various offices Caden visits throughout the film, remind me so much of *Beau Is Afraid*, which is only interesting—since *Beau Is Afraid* came after—because of both of their apparent relationship with Tati and *Playtime*, that is, two different directors, at very different points in their careers, apparently drawing on a film in such a way that they depict a sort of ruined metropolis the same way. In Aster's film, the absurdity and the comedy are cranked far higher, but that seems appropriate to its moment, coming out around the Covid-19 pandemic. For Kaufman, descending from what must've been the weird blur of *Being John Malkovich*, *Adaptation*, and *Eternal Sunshine of the Spotless Mind*, there's certainly a sense of some maturity, such that the surrealism is without commentary or direct referent to our world—these are human stories, or rather, this is the human story being told, with no jagged edges; such that, though *S.N.Y.* could certainly be called messy, I don't think it's an accusation that actually holds up when watching it. For all the apparent dissonances between this and our stable, logical world, watching it there aren't moments that make me feel like I'm not grounded in that world. The woman, as it turns out, is dropping off a key for "Ellen Bascomb," at Adele's apartment, so she asks him if he's Ellen.

Minute 71

"Yes, I'm Ellen." The music is heavy, moody, but Hoffman's delivery of the line is just magnificent. Ellen, as it turns out, is Adele's cleaning lady, so Caden, who's dressed arguably close to a cleaning lady in a heavy sweater vest, a white dress shirt, large glasses, heavy-looking black shoes, and black khakis—

admittedly, this is biased by where this aspect of the film goes, and as I wrote it try as I might I couldn't *make* the description sound more cleaning lady-like than I did, but with his hair longer, hunched over the toilet bowl, intently focused on his scrubbing, that's how he strikes me—now assumes the role of Ellen Bascomb, an aged cleaning lady. One can't really impose one's sense of what the music ought to be over what we're given, but I will acknowledge a dissonance here between the slight humor and arguably warm beauty of this moment, counterpointed by long, mournful notes that feel like the kind of music we might hear in a dramatic TV series after a love interest has parted ways and one sees the other working at a coffee shop or something. Writing it out I can see the logic of it—Caden is, after all, in his ex-wife's apartment; the only reason for his being there that he can find *is* work—but it's one of those aspects of *S.N.Y.* that I think often reads as *only* sad for so many viewers, which feels slightly unfortunate. Again, what's happening strikes me as slightly funny, and arguably warm and beautiful, and the music in this single minute feels slightly at odds with that; so of course it could always be that I'm experiencing the film dumbly. Of course, that could always be the case.

Minute 72

Afterwards he leaves, presumably boarding the same bus as Ellen Bascomb though the reality of that versus the sense of it feels at odds. He returns home, where Claire is, and it's unclear where Barnathan is. Claire accuses him of smelling weird, of wearing lipstick, and there's a warm bit of *Honeymooners*-style humor, or rather the setup feels *Honeymooners*-y, where the execution is all Kaufman: Claire says he smells like he's menstruating, though her delivery almost feels like it was a random word picked from the ether to characterize his smell—Freud would insist this is the thing she definitely meant to say, then, but I don't agree—and Caden says he doesn't know what she means, and Claire begins the classic sitcom wife routine of shutting him out with terse replies, "You tell me," she says, to her director-husband who smells like mold and cleaning products and possibly like he's menstruating who doesn't understand why he smells like he's menstruating, "I dunno," she delivers pitch perfectly behind a book at the breakfast table. It's sad, of course, the ways in which these love interests fall by the wayside in Caden's life, and I don't mean to imply she's simply functioning here as a comedic foil to the weird saga he's entering in late life. In a way it's like they change, and they grow, while Caden wants to change, and wants to grow—even pushing himself now into a cleaning lady's person with real commitment—but simply can't because of the gray weight of his consciousness. There's also, of course, the sense of his throwing himself into his paternal duties with zeal, a bit like Mrs. Doubtfire, looking for any way back into that past existence, but even this feels unmoored from such a clean interpretation, undergirded as it is by a murk of real humanity and experience, rather than the mere window dressings of a family dramedy.

Minute 73

Umberto Eco, in *The Open Work*, seeks to classify a mode of artwork that I think Caden finds himself creating in the warehouse in *S.N.Y.* The work, then, is an open work. Eco opens with examples from music, wherein Stockhausen, Berio, Pousseur, and Boulez created works that emphasized choice in the individual performer, introducing structure, with elements of randomness or openness that in some way enhance the experience. He brings in Joyce, whose "Wandering Rocks" chapter in *Ulysses* amounts to a tiny universe that can be viewed from different perspectives: the last residue of Aristotelian categories has now disappeared. Joyce is not concerned with a consistent unfolding of time or a plausible spatial continuum in which to stage his characters' movements."[10] The unwieldy nature of the Work for Caden seems to reflect this. He has welcomed in performers, and gives them notes, and direction, but then lets them enact what he's given them, and doesn't overly focus on any on particular; instead he adds, and adds, and compounds. He gives Claire, who's fed up with Caden, since the lines with him have been blurred, and she's aging, and he's brought Sammy Barnathan, this strange man, to play him, a note stating "You think you might be gay," when she and Barnathan are seemingly fighting a fight that she's simultaneously sort of having with Caden. The thing, then, has begun revolting on him, and the situation feels as if it's become too open. Too much possibility has been introduced, and thus Caden has veered considerably from Adele's admonition. He's embraced the open possibility of saying so much, giving the work such potential for vulnerability and expression of humanity, that he's run into the conundrum of perhaps saying nothing. What's effective, though, or affecting, is Caden is realizing it, and thus Kaufman is cognizant of these lines, of veering too far into openness, and Caden, at the end of this minute, standing with his hand on his hip, looks like a determined professor of logic, an aged modern Wittgenstein, frustrated and confused but determined to go forth, to figure this out.

Minute 74

As the film progresses, the recency of the actual lived experience compared with its performance in the work becomes compressed, separated here by only a scene of a minute or so, and it's interesting because it doesn't feel yet like it's exhausted the potential of exploring this subject, or rather, this mode of operating for a film, and by extension this mode of making art. There is, of course, a danger in dramatizing one's life and experience, but it feels more as if the film is trying to explore that, both its benefits and its limits—the fight when Caden handed Claire the "You think you might be gay" note highlighted this—and what might prove so alluring for an artist in this pursuit. One aspect of such immersive autofixation—for Caden, in this case, not Kaufman—can be a richness, the richness of Proust, that's probably not accessible by any other mode in my estimation. Someone—I might have read it, but if I did I can no longer find it; it might've been a professor, but I just can't remember anymore—referred to the power in Proust being that it lets us *look twice at life*. To me, this is one of the highest achievements of any artwork, that it can give the audience these moments of pausing, watching some repeated act of our days with new eyes, and enrich them in such a way that only this kind of artwork can. This is, I think, the allure for Caden, and in this scene, when Sammy-Caden returns home, and the argument ensues that ended with Claire mumbling "I dunno" behind her book at the breakfast table, he's observing sweetly, and seriously, trying to understand his own experience. The other side of it, the more addictive nature of it, is more akin to these families that endlessly cannibalize their own existence to maintain YouTube channels, documenting everything and coming to guide their family's life according to what will make for good content. In the realm of art, I'd argue we saw this in the Knausgaard *My Struggle* novels, which proved ruinous to his personal life, and took on an exhibitionistic quality as they progressed. Such moments likely occurred for Proust in turn, in fact they must have, which only shows that for each artist any choice brings with it sure positives and negatives that they must anticipate.

Minute 75

The woman to play Hazel (Emily Watson) shows up as the fight is ramping up, but it's a different fight from the one we saw happen between the actual Caden and Claire. Claire decides she's leaving, really leaving, to perform in *Needleman in a Haystack*, and Caden seems bothered by her leaving, but not to such an extent that he'll fight for it. There's a nice bit of comedy when Claire says, "I want you out of the apartment. The real one, you can keep this one," before storming out. Again, both the literal and the metaphorical weight of this situation, in terms of the toll it's taken on Caden and everyone surrounding him, is brutal. This is the side of the artist-genius narrative we usually only see in small moments between triumphs; screaming ex-wives with neglected children are present only to pave the way to proud achievements when the whole village supporting the artist-genius looks on in awe. Here it's different; it's both smaller, without the high dramatics and romance of other narratives, and far larger, as these are the experiences of their lives.

Minute 76

Caden tries, finally, to go after her, but half-heartedly. Hazel's already on the phone before she's out the door ordering a Claire replacement. This is almost certainly my reading into the situation, but it's tempting to look at this as a critique of abundance in the life of the artist, or the weird too-open constraints that might present themselves to an artist if given the means to do absolutely anything. "Too-open constraints" is, of course, a problem, but it's precisely what I mean since almost any artist's life will illustrate that scenarios of great opportunity, abundance, freedom, be they financial, circumstantial, or tied to some kind of reception—that is, the public suddenly cares in massive numbers, etc.—inevitably result in work that can be meandering, half-hearted, unfulfilling, and most especially in the cases of novelists who lug around hulking tomes for decades, unfinished. Caden's open work might not call for a conclusion, certainly, but since he persists in compounding and compounding there's certainly a sense of when the reward of having put the final touch on the work might arrive. This, too, however, in narratives of artists and writers of unfinished works they lug around for decades, becomes the new reward; they don't finish it because it's giving them something they can't get anywhere else. We see Caden, afterwards, in Claire's real apartment, gathering his things. She's swinging on a wooden swing off the kitchen, going over lines with an actor. She's laughing, smiling, finally enjoying herself. She's aged, but nothing like Caden, who from now until the end of the movie becomes brutalized by time. The minute ends with Caden standing at her door, formerly his door, listening to her laugh with the actor, other friends in the apartment, continuing on, a new fixation.

Minute 77

The scale of what Caden is constructing in the work, inside the warehouse, though often only implied, given the limitations of what entirely conveying such a thing would entail, is growing more and more staggering. It isn't the kind of thing that feels as if we're being put on, either, where the implied largeness of something in a film is expected to be sufficient to actually convey that. As the film progresses, we actually start to feel that largeness, the structures being built inside the warehouse, things seen briefly and deeply and then never seen again. We see Caden leave the apartment building, and look up, and almost instantly see the recreation of this moment inside the warehouse, but the wall outside of her apartment isn't finished, and as they're performing Caden, frustrated, says "This is a lie," asking his production designer to "wall it up," which is then done almost instantaneously, though the implication of time has been so firmly established by now, years passing in seconds, slipping away, that it doesn't feel hokey or forced. Another way of looking at the Proustian notion of "looking twice at life" is a nostalgia for the present, which I think about often but which is, writing it now, slightly embarrassing. Arguably, Caden's creation of this short-term memory ork embodies this desire, to hold onto the closest emotional phenomenon experienced, which ironically is mostly cut through by previous iterations of the same, such that he's perpetually trying to experience things that are becoming, to use Schopenhauer's phrase, mere representations of the actual experiences had, in Caden's perspective, years or potentially decades before. He's caught now, in the slipstream of immediate regurgitation of his life into the work, and any division between the two is now scant.

Minute 78

"It is perhaps times like these that one reflects on things past."—Olive's Diary, discovered by Caden when cleaning the apartment as Ellen Bascomb. A quieter version of the piano piece scattered throughout the film is playing, the really beautiful and slightly tragic though perfectly melancholic one, the embodiment of nostalgia as it's purely defined. It's heavy, but beautiful in this context, again a bit like the weird aspect of transgression throughout *S.N.Y.*, where somehow the logic of a father pretending to be a cleaning woman who never sees the people he cleans for—his former family—can get a note from his ex-wife about his potentially moving into a room in their place, and even a weird congratulations for his/Ellen's MacArthur Grant since Caden had acknowledged it in a previous writing but *as* Ellen; that all of this assembled together can reach a warmth and a beauty that this scene reaches is really something. Caden is older still, and shuffling throughout his life now more tentatively, and sadly, but he seems to feel, or perhaps it's we who feel, enlivened by the reading of the diary entry, the daughter now reflecting as the father has in the work, on games they'd play, pretending to be fairies, on walks they'd take.

Minute 79

The memories continue, as Robin Weigert's aged version of Olive narrates the diary, the memories of the game, bits and pieces we'd seen earlier, these small moments between a father and his daughter; the kind of things that, in retrospect, can weigh heavily on the father's consciousness, and for a child so young might not even be recorded. Caden is, and we are, breathing this in, this moment of deep intensity and connection with the failures of his life. What this—and what Proust—seems to be telling us—and we've cut now to Caden, far older, slowly walking into a weird kind of circular hospital room, brightly lit, which matters since Caden's were always so bleak, where we can see the older Olive, lying on a hospital bed, connected to machines, and she tells Caden that he needs to wear headphones with a microphone attached for her to hear him, so he puts them on, and sits down, beginning to cry, as Olive says, "I'm dying"—is that we can't know what these moments are going to be for us, can't anticipate the ways in which tragedy will fragment our existence, our relationships with our families, our partners, our children; and thus it is imperative to act in awareness of this fact, to not only let existence wash over us and wash us out of it clean.

Minute 80

The flower tattoos—this was something that, when I watched S.N.Y. for I think the third time, I wanted to get myself, the rose tattoos all over my body—it turns out, are infecting Olive, and killing her. Caden says that Maria is the one who did this to her. Olive responds that he's the one who left her, and both of them begin to weep, attempting to communicate across these divides not only of language but this willed misunderstanding on the part of Maria, who told Olive Caden was a homosexual, and that he'd deny it if confronted. I can imagine this moment happening in a soap opera, and perhaps the hospital bed, the lesbian lover/groomer, the closeted father who denies it—but who probably isn't, or at least hasn't put this idea into our heads, the audience—perhaps these elements are even meant to point to this sort of context. It's difficult to imagine that sort of an influence on Kaufman, but it feels safe to say that this is not the same sort of an absurd family dynamic and debacle we've gotten elsewhere in the film. It isn't played for laughter in the slightest. It feels heavy, and tragic, and, per Caden's earlier monologue, *fucked up*. There is a tendency for moments of real sincerity in narrative to cross the line into sentimentality, which puts an audience off. Here, however, there are so many strange constructions and artifices and apparatuses between these two characters that they've become as complex as the work, each with their means of coping with this impossibly tragic scenario, but each of them submitting too to the bodily call to weep. Perhaps, too, there is this misery in their not doing what we might've hoped throughout the film for them to do, for Caden to pick Olive up and hold her in his arms. The feeling, the heft we feel in watching them, I think, has to do with the fact that we won't be given that kind of thing, that resolution. It now appears that either of them might stand to be most redeemed, weirdly, by the work. It's possible I'm only ingesting Caden's madness.

Minute 81

Olive's wish is to forgive Caden before she dies. She says she has no time and needs him to ask for forgiveness for abandoning her "to have anal sex with his homosexual lover, Eric," and Caden doesn't protest, and here the extremity of their tears—or it might just be my own discomfort with the expression of raw emotion, I can't be sure—lets slight humor creep in, because although Caden submits to this extreme scenario, saying what she wanted to hear because she's his daughter and she's dying, and he's been deprived of this relationship for decades now, although he's done all of this, she still says "No," and both begin to weep more violently, Caden sadly muttering "Oh . . ." through tears. While these are characters in a made-up scenario and we're meant to believe they're presently at odds, it also feels like this submission to the tragedy and the absurdity of it somehow brings them together in their crying, though again I might just be projecting through my own discomfort. It works, too, and it seems like it shouldn't because the envelope keeps getting pushed and pushed; but it works, completely, such that it feels inevitable, like music.

Minute 82

Synecdoche, New York directed by Charlie Kaufman © Sony Pictures Classics 2008. All rights reserved.

The horror of this moment is not finally cut through by humor, however, not really. It's cut through in a surreal event, when Olive—who has died there on the bed, Caden crying next to her as Maria, who entered just as she's passing, holds Olive's head and says, "I hope you are happy, faggot," to which Caden repeats, "I'm not happy . . ."—she, or rather the tattoo on her arm, of these coiled and wilting, blackening red roses, drops a petal onto the hospital bed, which Caden quickly grabs. The piano music, mournful now, rises with the tears and the sorrow Caden's feeling, and Maria too, but in that act of desperately grabbing this final, strange, impossible piece of his daughter, whom he always deeply loved, there is beauty. It cuts then to an image painted by Adele of Olive, older, and she looks like a much darker piece of Lucian Freud, the red surrounding her and splotching her form accentuating the dark redness of the rose tattoos on either side of her body. Caden is at the gallery again, viewing the painting. Adele, too, has used her art to make sense of her existence, which is, finally, the great strength in what she did, the deeply personal nature of painting such tiny things, and sharing them with the world. Beautiful, rich, textured, expressive portraits of the people she loves in their most vulnerable states, rendered in miniature, such that they might be carried in one's pocket. Caden then sits on a stop on the street, which is growing more chaotic and more apocalyptic, which is simply like the world of any artist at any moment, in their estimation certainly. A naked man, wearing a dog collar, potentially on a leash, is walked down the street. A large army truck drives by. There's a man wearing a gas mask, seeming disorder everywhere. It feels like an exterior in a film about the end of the world, the setup for some figure waking up in a hospital bed alone, but feels far more connected to our experience, even for its surreal moments, since *S.N.Y.* has seemingly always attempted to accept the logic of human life, just slightly skewed.

Minute 83

"It's about everything." It now looks as though they are constructing a warehouse inside of the warehouse for the work. A shift in the music, to what I'm mentally classifying as a kind of Thomas Newman-y "plotting and scheming" register, immediately uplifts things, as does Sammy Barnathan, who observes a map of the warehouse, which indicates they're now at work on "Warehouse 2," and Barnathan peruses his actors on the street, which is now inside the first warehouse, and screams at two of them that what they're doing is not about "dating. It's about death!" He's just wonderful to watch. Caden and Hazel are following, and Caden says that in fact it is about dating, about death, about Everything, and Hazel scribbles it frantically into her notes.

Minute 84

The work, being now seemingly in the days near to not completion, exactly, but its more functioning, distilled state, which carries it now independent of the real Caden's influence, can also now playfully *mise en abyme* itself, with Caden observing Caden observing Caden, Hazel observing Hazel, and each of these iterations treating their work with the utmost seriousness, yet still their playful humanity. They are each old, of course, as our anchoring Caden is now old, and thus there's a sweetness to this, like an avant-garde theater production being put on in a home for senior citizens—budding romances brew, little comments on new additions, changes, the kids, and so on and so on. It feels entirely astounding that the range of emotions over the past few minutes of the film—to say nothing of the whole of *S.N.Y.*—could exist in concurrence, could logically somehow relate with and connect with and ensue from one another, and yet we now almost have the sense that we're contributing to Caden's work, which is the fundamental reality of any film—just think, for instance, of the sheer pleasure one feels when Kurt Russell smiles at us over his car in *Death Proof*, or Ferris Bueller addresses us directly—but in a truly open work film such as this it's more significant. Our emotional engagement with this subject matter is being rewarded in real-time now, and our connection to these characters, absurdly reiterated again and again, feels now as warm as the feeling might be in seeing our own grandparents, the foibles of our aged kin, play out in their back and forth, their picking nits, their attempts at constructing and reconstructing their small edifices of their remnants—largely in memory—of their worlds.

Minute 85

"Hazel . . . what do you think of this title? Unknown, Unkissed, and Lost."
"Meh."

Caden, before this, asks for the façade of Adele's building to be built, apparently in just a few days, which is incredible, though his builder/set designer looks extremely put upon, and ought to be considering all he's done in however much time has transpired since the work began. He returns to Adele's exhibition, to find a painting of the real Ellen Bascomb, who's partly nude, and then we're back in the warehouse, or warehouse 2—it isn't clear—where he's interviewing actresses who might perform the part of Bascomb. This is where we get this bit of dialogue, when Hazel's come over with the woman, strikingly similar to the painting, played wonderfully by Dianne Wiest. In a way, to refer again to one of Eco's examples of an open work, Bascomb/Weems will provide a kind of partial closure to the loop Caden's life thus far has opened, à la *Finnegans Wake*, and a good number of writers have already speculated about her primacy in this story, the ways in which she seemingly rounds everything out—she's led, in turn, to theorizing about the film, which sees her as the potential anchoring perspective for *S.N.Y.*, that is, everything we're watching is conjured up in the real Ellen's mind; though open-ended narratives, and certainly open works, often prompt an audience/reader/listener to such theorizing, it's a temptation I mostly try and resist, simply because I find the notion of "solving" works of art I love has a deadening effect on some of that love, though I might certainly be in the minority here. There's the interesting question of the money, which on the one hand seems as though it certainly would have dried up by now—of course this is a pathetic concern, and not one I happen to be overly concerned with, but so immersing myself in this manner has brought about these littler questions I might otherwise not consider for very long. I think in part the setup right now, at 01:26:33, with Caden seated at his desk, surrounded by papers, schematics, folders, files, and Hazel, looking at Millicent Weems/Ellen Bascomb in front of him, speaks to this dimension slightly. He's meticulous, which is also implied by his conversation with his builder/set designer—he gives him pictures, which we didn't see him take, and they're extensive, "stalker"-ish—and this kind of thing adds to the overall sense of something that feels essential now, to the narrative, which is how seriously Caden is taking the work still. It's possible to push something into such an extreme of absurdity that people simply can't hold onto it. I'd argue that sometimes the lyrics of a songwriter like Robert Pollard do this. Guided By Voices/Pollard are incredibly prolific, sometimes releasing multiple albums per year, and a great deal of the music is absolutely fantastic. The lyrics, often absurd, surreal, informed by Pollard's love of strange 1960s pop, often veer just a bit too far into strangeness and, if you're listening for the lyrics, can lose you just a bit. Brian Eno, as a counterpoint to this, both in terms of restraint—that is, not releasing as much stuff—and in terms of anchoring his work with elements that ground an audience, seems more reflective of what Kaufman is doing now in S.N.Y., and what Caden's view of the Work really is. This also abuts the conversations often had around art fundamentally. Is it "useless," per Wilde, "a game," per Cortazar? If it's these things—and, granted, Cortazar was referring directly to literature in his quote, but I don't think it's a problem to extend it to art, or at the least narrative film like S.N.Y.—where does that leave its creators in terms of their seriousness about it? Their audiences? Will society simply laugh at them, or disregard what they do because of it? Adele, in S.N.Y., looks like an "artist." She acts like an "artist." The messy hair. The sexual meanderings. The time in

Europe. The paint-stained clothes. Caden, on the other hand, and presently especially, looks like a put-upon businessman. An accountant, or an architect, worn down by age, and work, and time. In his way, then, this is how he's made sense of his relationship to something that might strike his potential audience as absurd, or certainly his critics as absurd— *useless, a game*, etc.—that he is treating utterly seriously. That he is completely devoted to. That he is living his life for in every respect now.

Minute 86

Weems is standoffish, but "weirdly close" to what Caden's picturing for the character, so she's brought on, and quickly drastically changes her appearance, or rather, has her appearance changed, for the role. Perhaps it's a gray wig that she's given, and a loose-fitting crewneck sweater in a purply pink, with some sort of stuff embroidered all over it. She looks, in short, like a cleaning lady. She looks, in short, like Ellen Bascomb. This is the problem, again, with theories. It's suddenly very tempting, and very easy, remembering the different theories I've read about *S.N.Y.*, to start thinking about it along those lines, because I've just mentioned them, and because once you're informed about something like this, it's such an effective lens that your experience of the thing being theorized is sort of kept at bay. This is one work of art that I do not want kept at bay, nor do I want my experience of it to be kept at bay. I would almost go so far as to say that we should introduce a moratorium on theories about works of art for fifty or so years, just because they prove so ruinous to the experiences of those works of art for so many people. They might not feel that their experiences are being ruined, but if someone tells you X is really a metaphor for Communism, or Y is really a film about how the director was assaulted, and those things aren't pretty patently clear to someone, then the unfortunate reality is those things will begin being about those things for people who've encountered those theories, unless of course they've already got their own substantive theory to account for the whole endeavor, in which case I'm sure they'll tell us shortly. It might even run counter to the critical impulse in general, because I don't believe works of art necessarily benefit from excessive explanation. I say that, in this context, of writing a text about a film minute-by-minute, but I hope that what I've managed to do thus far, and will continue to try to do, is not simply *explain*, or reduce, or contain *S.N.Y.* I don't want any of those things. I don't wish to be smarter than *S.N.Y.*, or Charlie Kaufman, or more interesting, or a better writer or anything. I am interested in the film itself, and I do believe in a certain mode of critique that embraces the notion that responding honestly to something, or not even responding, simply *talking* about something that you're passionate about, or that affects you, can be a wonderful thing, can be as vital as someone telling you a direct story about their experience, because essentially that's what I'm doing.

Minute 87

The work, in its recurrence, its recursion, seems to transcend the pathetic nature of simply treading over the same ground again and again anxiously. They try, outside the door, Caden and Hazel—the real Caden and the real Hazel—and Ellen, and the actual woman (I think?) from when Caden actually visited Adele's apartment and got this part of the work started, the one who wanted to give him the key. Caden hears Adele's voice inside the apartment, and it affects him in a surprising way. This is what I mean about its transcending mere obsessive poring. Because of the recursive nature of the work, which in turn is contained inside *S.N.Y.* proper, I suddenly feel as a viewer the love that Caden feels for Adele, which frankly I don't know that I felt until this moment in the film. He looked, as self-obsessed and busy and normal fathers and husbands tend to, as though his love for her in the beginning was probably somewhat starved, or at least this is what we're given. Adele was starved, of course, for something, and hence she seeks out Maria, and this great change for her existence. And then she cries, and it's entirely unexpected how affecting it feels. She doesn't want to be doing what she's doing then, or doesn't want this—or that—to be her life. Now, Caden—and the music—is uplifted by mistakenly thinking he hears her voice—it's a recording, an impossibility, which is nicer for it—and it takes him back to something, and there's almost a feeling as warm as the return, in *Fargo*, of Norm and Marge to their bed, at the end, which I've never been able to watch without wanting to run to my wife, which feels to me the purest distillation of the best case scenario for any artist-husband/father. Caden is breaking down. Weems/Bascomb needs help with her lines. They are, in their ways, returning.

Minute 88

There's a nice little bit of small fussiness in Caden now, fixating on little aspects of the work, and it's treated with seriousness, with earnestness, because all of them still believe in the Work. He tells an actor he's worked with since the Miller reimagining "People don't walk like that," which feels like it's happened before, but I've watched the film and rewatched this minute so many times it's not exactly clear if that's the case. Instantly, the actor tries a different walk, attempting to walk more like himself—an impossibility. He asks the actress playing Hazel where Sammy and Hazel are, only to find they're flirting standing against a large structure. He tells Sammy the real Hazel doesn't exist for him, so if he wants to like a Hazel it needs to be the actress playing Hazel. It's a bit like he can feel this thing slipping through his fingers, and also, of course, a likely bit of jealousy at Sammy's natural confidence and propensity for acting like a bit of a sadistic cuckolder. All the same, he directs his actors, giving notes, and organizes his world. I recently read D. T. Max's *Every Love Story Is a Ghost Story*, his biography of David Foster Wallace, and I can't help but be reminded of the weird trouble that might occur in an artist's life when they're deep into a project that seems to have no ending in sight, and their only way out of it is through. In both cases, a MacArthur Grant does sort of inaugurate the beginning of this larger project, and in both cases it's almost too much of an uplift, though in Wallace's real-life case he wound up mostly giving the money away to friends in AA because it weighed on him—and really, in the case of a novelist, aside from some IRS texts and courses he took in accounting (that were likely free since he was faculty) to research for *The Pale King*, it's not like he'd have something like the work to pour everything into anyway. It does make me wonder, since *Adaptation* sort of opens up the mind to speculating along these lines, whether some of this, too, is Kaufman himself working toward the end of the film. There's still around half an hour left, but this sense that Caden's tidying things up, going through possibilities for names; that there are people in *S.N.Y.* asking about an audience, about when the thing will open—he seems to be in search of an ending.

Minute 89

They talk about it further, and it doesn't seem as if it's deeply bothering Caden—he actually laughs—but he does begin to recognize that he's not the center of these people's universe exactly, that they're trying to live lives even while devoting themselves to the work. We also get that they're on "Equity Break," with ten minutes before they've got to get back to work, which further helps the whole thing have more shape, since sometimes it can seem as if they're simply *always* there, always working on it, without too much shape to any of it.

Caden then gets a call that his mother has died in a home invasion in Schenectady, so we're back at a funeral, where we do see Caden's father standing a few people away from him, and in the next scene he's asking the woman playing Hazel if, in fact, they were standing by his father at the funeral. She doesn't know what he looks like, and Caden informs her that "He's dead." There does seem to be this shift in life when suddenly the primary social events one attends are funerals, and one becomes rather fixated on the dead, on dying. We aren't seeing things from Caden's perspective when we see his father, however, because we're also seeing Caden to understand how close they're standing together. He isn't simply haunted, then. He isn't haunted, and he isn't also now involved in some kind of paranoiac thriller like *The Game*. The father is not really there, then, or if he is, it's only in the sense that Millicent Weems is really Ellen Bascomb, "and so on and so on" to quote Slavoj Žižek. With the death of both parents, too, and the sense of one's finality in life, they say that one undergoes significant change, heavy realizations, another kind of whenever-life crisis for Caden's third act.

Minute 90

For a long time I only really knew Emily Watson from *Red Dragon*, which is a strange film to know Emily Watson from exclusively. It's a limiting role, I've realized, from this, from *Breaking the Waves*. She's far more dynamic than she's often given the chance to be, at least in American films I've seen with her since. In this, she's playing an actress playing Hazel, and doesn't come across as particularly obsessed with acting as a devotion; she's not like Claire, for instance, or certain other characters throughout *S.N.Y.* In this minute, she doesn't say much of anything. She sits, talking with Caden at the funeral, drinking. She observes her director, this man who's just lost his father. She lets him talk, because people need to talk when they've just lost their father. He talks mostly about her, Tammy, and the ways in which she's comforting to have with him—he'd wanted to bring the real Hazel, but she couldn't come, so he thought of her as the "next best thing," which he explains he doesn't mean to be insulting. It's quiet, and subdued, I'd say, rather than being aggressively depressing—like the adult world I use to imagine, when our parents would bring us over to friends' houses to play with their kids in the basement while they'd drink, everyone wearing suits, lots of perfume and cologne in the air, everyone drinking something alcoholic, and everyone largely quiet, subdued, which is probably a more apt descriptor for the one funeral I've attended so far as an adult, my father's.

Minute 91

I've often felt that "setup" scenes in films are things I'd like to live within for a very long time, certainly longer than filmmakers will ever put us in them. I mean the scenes like when Anton Chigur is wounded, in No Country for Old Men, so he blows up a car so that he can get into a pharmacy to get the good medication and treat himself. He's holed up in a motel room, removing fragments from a shotgun blast from his leg, hidden from his enemy in Llewelyn Moss, and the sense of the potential there is overwhelming. They usually involve preparation, which this minute sort of does, though of course it's nothing like a hitman tending to his wounds to continue on his path of violence. There's just a nice feeling—not unlike the feeling you'd really have, were you sitting at a funeral with the woman playing your assistant, talking about your real assistant and the man who's playing you, what they're doing, what's going on—that's never explored for much longer than that. Though Tammy, who Caden calls "Yammy" here, doesn't say much, seems nervous, is straddling this weird line between respecting her director and being her real, honest self—which feels like sort of a "fun aunt"—and in that sense of her restraint there's yet more of that palpable potential that's really compelling to focus on.

Minute 92

There's a moment of strange violence when Caden and Tammy walk by Caden's parents' room, where initially Caden said that she could sleep. Blood is swathed on the floor by the bed, violent thick lines of it, pictures knocked down, blood on the bed too where his mother must've been sleeping. It seemed as though the expediting device of her death was the thing for the film right now, but the nature of her death matters, it all does. She was killed in a home invasion, and by the looks of it was stabbed, slashed, perhaps shot. It seems most tempting to read this in line with the depictions of the "world outside" we've seen throughout the film, the moments outside of both warehouses, which are really one warehouse, where the work is contained. Framed photographs are on the ground, the details briefly lingered over as though we've momentarily shifted into the immediate aftermath on an episode of *Law and Order: SVU* or something. Caden says that he figured somebody might've cleaned it up, and Tammy asks "Who?" the weird implication being I guess Caden, which might reflect the fact that his parents, his family, have really been as adrift from his life, from the work, as Olive and Adele, excepting of course that they provide his subject matter. They go to Caden's old room, and again this idea of returning, recurring, and again this idea that as we get older, we become as helpless as we were as children. He says he'll sleep on the couch at first, and Tammy says she thought he'd be sleeping with her. We've been thinking this, too, ambiently, since it's a funeral, and the film has set up a precedent there, I suppose, and there's always a sense of tension when Caden's with a new woman. What's funny is she doesn't beat around the bush at all, follows this up saying *it's just sex*, and commingled with the childhood bedroom stuff it's of course tempting to read the whole thing psychoanalytically, but there's never an indicator we should read this as something that's only fantastical; or if there is, it feels somehow more in line with the existence of the film to read what's happening in it as what's happening in it. It's not as if Kaufman's directing under the tyrannical rule of Stalin or something. She gets undressed, and Caden comments on the disparity between their comforts with this, that being beautiful must help, that he can't imagine it. He's ashamed. His head is down.

Minute 93

It's a bit like the end of *Eyes Wide Shut*, when all that neuroses has played out in such lush, paranoiac, slow-moving detail, every stone turned over, every thought analyzed and reanalyzed and explored and interrogated, and the fundamental thing that Tom Cruise's character needs is for his wife to say we need "To fuck." Caden is unsure. Anxious and unsure. Freaking out internally and feeling the loneliness he's felt for however long welling up for him in this horrible way, in front of this woman he barely knows, who he finds beautiful, who's standing comfortably naked before him, telling him that she wants to fuck. He doesn't give over entirely to his loneliness. He doesn't let it ruin the situation entirely. He lets her take some control of their interaction, because she's composed, and she's understanding, and she knows what she wants out of this situation, that it isn't some big complex problem to be analyzed and reanalyzed. He needs connection. He needs to get off, sure. It's crude to put it that way but it's a situation that seemingly calls for a crudeness, a human-level thing, a gut-level thing, just like *Eyes Wide Shut*. These are the twin forces seemingly balancing out the world. Not necessarily between the masculine and the feminine, but between the bodily and the mental, the cerebral and the brutish. He mostly keeps his head down, working at his tie. She tells him to take off his clothes, that "fucking might help" his state. He gives himself over to this because he doesn't have any other ideas that'll help.

Minute 94

He tells her that he wishes he could be pretty like her, and it's a moment of vulnerability we seldom get from characters like Caden Cotard, that is, characters so firmly immersed in their thinking, their misery, their sense of duty to a certain kind of art-making that drives them in all things. To suddenly have such a character pivot, to share that he sometimes wishes he could be pretty, that maybe he'd have been better at being a girl, this kind of vulnerability can connect people; the kind of vulnerability we get in Hemingway's *The Garden of Eden*, for example, where both the myth of the author and the myth of the author in text are undercut but the swapping of gender roles at night, and the apparent necessity of this to sustain the rest of the relationship. In that case it's about a marriage, in *S.N.Y.* it's about Caden's relationship with himself. There are some things that only get fully experienced when they're expressed vulnerably, especially to a stranger. In *Garden of Eden*, itself a kind of open work since we've never seen the entirety of the text, and unless we can visit Hemingway's archive may never, the ending features a destruction of an artwork, commingled with this relationship, the apparent ruination of an artist (this case, a writer); and yet, it isn't treated that way, it's almost viewed optimistically, this act of destroying, because the writer, David Bourne, has found perspective. In the morning after, they drive back together, Tammy smoking and drinking coffee, looking every bit the miserable couple returning from a funeral.

Minute 95

There are these intricacies in the production of theater that, though Caden's work is now entirely outside the purview of any extant theater production I'm familiar with, are still being observed, which again highlights Caden's commitment to this thing he's doing—he is not simply buying time, just as Kaufman is not simply filling out this film, though both of them, of course, have grown massive, and our perception may be that this is unwieldy, chaotic, these simple gestures again are anchoring to the entire experience. Likely because Caden and Tammy/Hazel slept together, Tammy/Hazel seems to feel a confidence now, so as Sammy/Caden is walking with Tammy/Hazel, commenting on the performances of the actors behind doors—there's a hilarious moment when Sammy/Caden tells Roland he's doing good and immediately whispers to Tammy/Hazel "We need to fire him"—Caden and Hazel are walking behind them commenting on what they're doing, and eventually Tammy/Hazel turns to talk to Caden about a notion that's crossed her mind, that there might be a conflict between Sammy/Caden and Caden over Tammy/Hazel and Hazel, primarily Hazel, who both of them have expressed interest in, Hazel seemingly preferring a more intimate relationship with Sammy/Caden than Caden. By the end of it she's got the stem of her glasses in her mouth, eyes glowing, standing behind the actual Hazel, looking right at Caden with a knowingness that's fun, a camaraderie, while Hazel looks at Caden as though he must know how ridiculous this is, and how it should not be pursued. We can see the Work growing, which might otherwise feel like a worrisome thing, but if we're able to remain awash in the experience of *S.N.Y.* it doesn't honestly feel that way. Because of Caden's determined demeanor in all of this, his earnest relationship to everything they're doing, and his genuine reactions to these situations, such things wind up feeling entirely necessary. Better still, they feel inevitable.

These two quotes, from Antonin Artaud, in *The Theater and Its Double*, I think, characterize the sensation pretty perfectly:

> Theater of Cruelty means a theater difficult and cruel for myself first of all. And, on the level of performance, it is not the cruelty we can exercise upon each other by hacking at each other's bodies, carving up our personal anatomies, or, like Assyrian emperors, sending parcels of human ears, noses, or neatly detached nostrils through the mail, but the much more terrible and necessary cruelty which things can exercise against us. We are not free. And the sky can still fall on our heads. And the theater has been created to teach us that first of all.
>
> I cannot conceive any work of art as having a separate existence from life itself.

Minute 96

Again, the further afield an artist gets from reality, or not reality exactly, but the recognizable elements of lived experience for most of us, the closer—in my view—they need to hew to certain elements to give the work elements that level it out. I mentioned Brian Eno as an exemplar of this, and with him sometimes it's something as simple as a title, i.e., *Music for Airports* coming from the artist behind *Taking Tiger Mountain By Strategy* sets us up as much as it can for a further example of musical abstract expressionism—more Rothko than Pollock—something "as ignorable as it is interesting,"[11] an ambition that seems to articulate perfectly this tension that Kaufman needs to establish for *S.N.Y.*, where we're now decades into the work, and Caden and Hazel are having a conversation about Sammy/Caden, and Caden's told that Derek left Hazel because of Caden, and Sammy/Caden is offering her comfort, inside the warehouse, which is hulking, citylike, large enough to seemingly contain a recreation of itself inside itself, stretching the architecture of fiction à la *House of Leaves*, but we're freed up from thinking over logic because we're watching these two aged persons have a conversation that's difficult for them, and like most conversations there are at least three conversations happening; Caden's, Hazel's, and the actual words being spoken between them. Caden, for his part, complains that he'll have to let go of the actor who played Derek, hurting Hazel, who seems on the edge of tears.

Minute 97

Caden and Hazel's relationship, since he convinced her to join the work, in the aftermath of their failed relationship, has felt of course awkward, of course strained. This interaction, then, initially sad and ugly as it gets, seems to be bringing them somehow back together, likely not as mates, but as elderly friends who not only understand one another but are interested in understanding one another. Hazel had Caden's number, leading up to this, being hurt by him in an intimate context, with Caden groveling after her afterwards, convinced she'd become the one-who-got-away, but in a strange way they now convincingly need one another, not just as director and producer, but again, as friends, that rarest thing as one drifts further into age. Caden acknowledges here, too, that they have "enormous budgetary concerns," which I believe is the first actual mention of the money question per the Work in the film, though as previously noted it's something obviously on Caden's mind, being as meticulous and orderly as he is. There is a deep pleasure in being known, really known, by those one cares about; which can often mean revealing a lot of ugliness, and fucking up, and doing things we regret, and for those of us lucky enough to have those people stick around, the aftermath, where we are known, and we are even understood, can provide us, like Caden, something essential to continue on with our lives.

Minute 98

There's a moment when their intimacy seemingly comes
back, but it's not clear whether they're talking about the
work or themselves, when Hazel says, "What are we doing?"
and Caden answers honestly, "I don't know," and then they
lean in, simply, and share a kiss. Whether or not this is a
rekindling of their romance probably doesn't matter exactly,
since we quickly cut to see Sammy Barnathan, standing
seemingly beneath some bleachers, watching the two of them
and crying violently. A slow, mournful song begins to play,
and we cut to Caden showing Hazel the exterior of the hotel
where he'd watched Hazel return to her family that day in
New York when she'd said she couldn't return to him, that
she'd moved on, that she was happy. We see the balcony ledge
where Caden almost leapt off, and with the music playing
it feels uneasy, and briefly the thought occurs that perhaps
Caden is going to reveal to Hazel that he'd attempted suicide
here, or that perhaps he'll attempt it again when we cut to
a shot of Sammy, the heights of the warehouse in soft focus
behind him, crying and first calling out softly to Caden, softly,
then louder, trying to get his attention, trying to get him to
watch what he's going to do. He's higher up than the ledge

where Caden attempted to jump, and now everyone's looking up at him. "I've watched you forever Caden, but you've never really looked at anyone other than yourself. So watch me. Watch my heartbreak. Watch me jump." He stands there, awkwardly, and Caden screams at him, extremely angry now, when Sammy turns and jumps, killing himself, screaming, "Hazel, I love you!" With no sound as his body hits the ground, breaks through what must be stage construction, and the rest of them are on the ground looking at them, with Caden still angry, screaming, "I didn't jump, Sammy! A MAN STOPPED ME BEFORE I JUMPED. *GET UP!*" But Sammy's dead, lying on the ground with blood coming from his face, Hazel weeping on the ground as Caden stands there, still angrily asserting that he didn't jump. This is another moment, for entirely different reasoning, where I felt I simply couldn't stop the film at the exact one-minute mark from the previous timecode because what was happening proved too intense, and Sammy's tragedy too sincere to simply cut and talk about whatever might be happening in leading up to his suicide. Because of his apparently sadistic nature in prior scenes, I think his heartbreak, and his decision to end his life—to go through with what Caden failed to do in similar circumstances—feels all the more awful, all the more real, like maybe his demeanor previously was largely a put-on, the strange coping mechanism of an avowed and outspoken stalker who's finally found the perfect context for what he was doing anyway. Again, I think of this notion of transgressing expectations in art. In something like Joachim Trier's *Oslo, August 31st*, a modern retelling of *Le Feu Follet* (*The Fire Within*) by Louis Malle—wherein it feels slightly less expected given it's the first, unless we've read *Will O' the Wisp* by Pierre Drieu La Rochelle first (which can't be many of us and certainly wasn't and still isn't myself)— we're confronted with the prospect of our protagonist's suicide almost immediately, such that whether or not he'll kill himself by the end feels almost beside the point, like the film is doing something other than simply test whether or not the circumstances of this person are going to lead to their death—though, writing it out, I'm realizing that's kind of exactly what it seems to be doing, but it's doing that so aggressively out of the gate, we're less inclined to feel too broken up over it; we've merely gone from worst to worst. Here, though, we have the suicide of a man who's gone from stalking a theater director to starring as that theater director, under his direction, in said theater director's masterpiece. We've gone from weird to horrendous, in other words, and the effect of it is really brutal, like witnessing the death of a local eccentric we've grown to love.

Minute 100

At the funeral, something strikes Caden, and we get a sort of reworking of Shakespeare's "All the world's a stage, and all the men and women merely players," when he tells Hazel that he knows "how to do it now," that "there are no extras," and that they'll each be given their due. It's a beautiful realization, delivered softly into Hazel's ear while the mournful music plays, and they bury Sammy, and we instantly cut to his recreation of this, inside the warehouse, as a part of the work, and he asks Hazel if she can understand what he was trying to impart to her in saying this. This impulse is something I'm familiar with, the sense of a kind of ethic in art-making of any kind, this idea of making art to serve, to tell the stories of everyone we can, to "give the mundane its beautiful due," per Updike, who for all of his drawbacks certainly got that impulse right. There's a Korean writer, Ko Un, whose *Ten Thousand Lives* attempts to contain brief accounts of every single person he's ever met. It's the impulse of Samuel Pepys, to suddenly begin meticulously documenting as much of his life as he might. The impulse of Robert Shields, the diarist, who at some point felt compelled to begin recording every single thing he experienced, in staggering, often fecal, detail. His diaries are housed at the library where I work, and I've taken days to go and pore over them, these snippets of life mere decades ago, these stories of the people he's encountered. Caden is feeling magnanimous, then, his work, likely directly in reaction to Sammy's accusations before his suicide, that Caden only wanted to look inward, at himself, it must now be directed outward, toward these people, to give them each their prominence. In watching the performance of what they'd just experienced, Hazel tells Caden "Come over tonight," and we cut to them at her home, an old couple in a burning house, discussing missing their children—there's a small laugh when Caden again can't remember his other daughter's name, though I might be reaching because I'm feeling mournful the film is nearing its end—and there's a new beauty they're arriving at. I neglected to mention, too, that Caden says "there are 13 million people in the world," and given the scenes depicting the outside world I'm wondering if this is as a result of some horrific event, or some sequence of horrific events. Initially I'd thought Caden mispronounced "billion," but the actor who follows as Caden says "million" too, which is just the kind of nagging detail that I feel tempted to fixate on even though so much of the film I'm able to let merely wash over me and try to appreciate it in simplest terms. It's curious. [This is me, offstage, continuing to think about this, gritting my teeth that I'm not a logician, but leaving you be because I'm sure you've got your own set of concerns arising from your viewing and I don't want to step on your toes. You're the lead, after all.]

Minute 101

"I wish we had this when we were young. And all those years in between." (Hazel)
[. . .]
"Yeah, the end is built into the beginning." (Ibid.)

There's more said, of course, but these moments stand out as Caden and Hazel sit together, their lives together

winding down, *S.N.Y.* winding down, and the story itself
and potentially the work winding down. There's a warmth
now, both to the firelight and to this moment, that didn't
seem to exist before, or if it did it was this misdirected sexual
energy—both of them did want that, and do, and it was
fun, and palpable, but they were sort of ships passing, as it
were, and their miscommunication drove them apart. They
are coming together in a more substantial mode now, where
they've become friends, first, after being briefly a tryst, and
failing at that, and these connections—the best friend who
fundamentally understands you, who you've fundamentally
loved in your way for as long as you can remember—seem to
cut through the bullshit of all living, all experience, like the
purest language or the purest music played just so. There is
regret, yes, bound up in wishing they could've had it then, but
neither of them was really ready, and they needed to live their
lives to want what they presently want. This is the impossible
aspect of the Will, for Schopenhauer, as well as its force, its
fundamental necessity in our living, that is, one can regret the
turns one's life took, because the thing we presently desire so
much, that we're willing toward so much, should've been there
all along, but we are subject to this thing, as Caden and Hazel
are—not one human animal escapes it, for even those that
take it into their own hands forever enact its Representation
for any witness—and thus it isn't lingered over, it's moved on
from, they are coming together, they are being there for one
another in impossible circumstances—they're all impossible—
and thus we get one of the fundamental theses of *S.N.Y.*, *the
end is built into the beginning*, that is, we've done this before,
and we'll continue doing this, the film loops, our narrative
loops, compounds on itself, grows as the Work grows—think,
again, of the mise en abyme of each of their experiences, little
Russian dolls of their lives extrapolating outward—and too
the return for both of them, Caden to the simpler comforts of
home, Hazel to the love of this man she's admired, and hated,
and loved. It's a statement of fact.

Minute 102

The simple embarrassments of growth, both of aging and of becoming oneself, in a relationship. They prepare to go to bed, and Caden warns that he might have difficulty, that he takes "a lot of pills," and of course these days we are all Caden, most of us we are all taking "a lot of pills," to become righted. He prepares what may be a CPAP machine, next to the bed, or oxygen, I'm not sure, and Hazel keeps telling him "It's okay," reassuring him and holding him, keeping him safe, more or less, from the fire, and the hellish world outside, and of course from the fundamental him that drives so many wedges throughout his life, that exacerbates his miseries and in the past would've ruined him with this embarrassment, strangled him and strangled this moment and turned him and the narrative inside out—all of it inside out.

Minute 103

"The Obscure Moon Lighting an Obscure World."
"I think it might be too much."
"Yeah probably."

It's difficult to remember now, but there's a sweetness in Caden telling Hazel his ideas for titles, and part of me hopes he's only told them to her, though I don't think that's true, and I don't know that I presently have it in me to look, or care in precisely the way I'd need to care to pursue such a thing. They're lying together, and Caden tells her his idea for a title, and given his demeanor there's almost a sense of anxiety that he'll get angry, or deeply depressed and troubled over this, but with his age he's mellowed a great deal, and he's able to laugh, and know that she's right, and know too his own sort of ridiculous nature, but not second-guess himself now—we're too far in, he's too far in, the both of them are simply too far in—and she doesn't try to tear down the whole house of cards either, she's as committed as she's ever been if not more so; and thus when it shifts, and we see Caden walking around her home quite frantically, seemingly the morning after, again the weight of it is tragic, almost too much, and yet somehow right for the two of them, this moment of incredible intimacy before something horrible has happened. At the end of the minute—I wanted to keep myself from playing more, to keep my word—we see a medical Q-tip, which I'm sure is just the brand of the swab it really is, and not this particular swab, since I'm sure some medical company makes it, shows black on its cotton, which points to Hazel's completion of her choice, way back when, of how she's to die.

Minute 104

Hazel dies, of course, from smoke inhalation, from living inside of the burning house. As these things will tend to do in the lives of artists, this prompts Caden to figure out the way that he's to do the work. He decides to change it so that it takes place over the course of a single day, "and that day will be the day before [Hazel] died. It was the happiest day of [Caden's] life." It's a wonderful, if bleak, reinterpretation of the open work model of *Ulysses*, which Joyce set on the day he and Nora Barnacle first had sex, the beginning of the blossoming of their relationship. In *S.N.Y.*, in part because we've seen Caden endure strange tragedy after strange tragedy, it sort of becomes clear to us that it's the best day of his life as well, to finally be understood. He wants to experience it again and again, as much as he can. We get all this from a message he's leaving for Hazel, after she's dead. We then see Caden prepping for the day's rehearsal, in the warehouse. He's got another idea for a title: *Infectious Disease in Cattle*, and as with most of his title reveals, the reaction is poorly received. He stands there, the living embodiment of a kind of lifelong sorrow, brushing his hand over the hair of a wig as an assistant talks with him, empathetically, or probably it's the wig designer, or makeup artist. There's a real kindness in this person standing with Caden, a warmth I'll sometimes feel from people who work in highly specific industries and who devote themselves to their work with a great deal of passion and who are largely misunderstood.

Minute 105

"Caden Cotard is a man already dead. He, um, he lives in a half world between stasis and antistasis, and time is concentrated. Chronology confused." (Millicent)

Millicent says this to Caden when he acknowledges they need a new Caden for his Hazel. She says she knows it's a "nontraditional casting," but as with Sammy's proposal to Caden to play Caden there's this moment of understanding, this moment that illustrates she's been researching the role, and feels driven, and wants to play him, that seems to be affecting him. It functions as a sort of thesis to the film, really, and one can almost imagine Charlie Kaufman giving it as a frustrated answer to confused funders for the project when they're wondering what he's been working on after however many months of not reading the script. This phrase, "already dead," is one that's always given me trouble. Crass, the seminal UK anarcho-punk band, had the song "You're Already Dead," which is probably the first place my mind goes, and then to Denis Johnson's strange, quietly drugged 1997 novel *Already Dead*. In its best iterations it seems to impart a kind of freedom, the removal of the need to behave as we've been programmed to by all of our lived days. The ridiculousness, too, of behaving in any other manner, considering we will die, as all will; and this is the reading of it that I most like. It gives me trouble, though, to think of it as a kind of resignation, a tossing up the hands in the face of the very real problem of existence, of trying to figure out how to be a person, and assuming everything is quite useless because in X number of years we'll merely be dead—which, of course, we will, as all will. I understand that this interruption, or this imposition, by Millicent, is one of the motivators people cite when thinking of her as the sort of mind of the film, the thinking from which *S.N.Y.* springs. Again, I can wholly appreciate this, but given my disinterest in what feels like an ideological approach to critique, it's something I'm consciously resisting—ideological because once one takes it to be The Thing, it becomes quite easy to simply slot any internal resistance we might have to it (i.e., original thinking) and be content with reading any adjacent things as more evidence of X. What follows, though, is quite exceptional, and it's the kind of thing that really lets work that takes on a meta direction survive, being more than mere navel-gazing. Commentary upon not just character, but on the nature of both what we're presently watching and what any audience of the work would be seeing, is something that helps an audience feel slightly less unmoored—or more moored, rather—from a recognizable narrative context, be it filmic or otherwise. There are endless examples of this, but two that always jump to mind from teaching are T. S. Eliot's "These fragments I have shored against my ruins," which simultaneously speaks to the process of writing *The Waste Land*, and the net effect of this funereal, appropriative, death-obsessed ode to Eliot's experience; and Kurt Cobain's "I'll start this off/Without any words," from "On a Plain," just one of many moments wherein the songwriting process seemingly exhausts itself, or Kurt Cobain just gets kind of bored with it all, and writes lyrics that comment on the songwriting process itself—he also does this on being a singer in a band, his audience, and other components of this exchange. "Time is concentrated. Chronology confused," and these are elements, of course, of what we're watching, but as it's stated they're elements of Caden, *because* he's "already dead," and because he's living in this half "world between stasis and antistasis." In the obvious sense he's our protagonist, he's the lens through which we've witnessed *S.N.Y.*, and thus not only will his "story" affect what we're watching, but his demeanor, his outlook, his mode of operating will affect the actual contours of what we're watching. The weird relationship with time, then, is sort of equivalent to the attempt of a Proust to expand his memory into the kind of thing we might daydream at our most romantic. Where Proust expands, because his medium allows for it, and his circumstance seems to call for it, Kaufman contracts, because of the medium of film, perhaps because of his circumstance, but certainly because of Caden's, where we're getting a substantial chunk of this character's life, perhaps its most impactful moments, and we need to get them relatively efficiently. There is also, I think, a connection here—"The end is built into the beginning," said Hazel—with Caden's family leaving him, his stuckness in this space, this hell he's found himself in for the past two hours—or two decades or more—and the way in which that reality has altered his consciousness. I say this as a husband and a father and someone who tries to write in turn, the weird range of emotions I've experienced is suddenly doused in sulfuric acid and tossed up high into the wind when I'm to spend a substantial amount of time away from my family. Thankfully it hasn't ever been in the same manner as Caden, but there's a weird psychological thing that seems to happen that I can only really equate to a kind of death, in that it never goes how you think it'll go— you'll never be excited, eating tubs of cereal in front of the TV and living like a bachelor again; at least I won't—and its effects are burrowy and strange.

Minute 106

This is maybe my favorite of the role changes in the film. Caden's response after Millicent tells him that he's "turned to stone" at this point in his life, his work, a simple "OK, sounds good," sets in motion a minor freakout of his assistant, who says he saw the work as "much more hopeful," and Caden lovingly shushes him, caressing his hand. We then cut to a performance of the funeral, where Caden had his revelation about the work, where we get to see Millicent/Caden directing, her approach is largely opposite Caden's—she's critical, gets up almost immediately and makes apparently significant changes, which again sends Caden's assistant into a minor freakout, but Tammy/Hazel provides a sort of shrug, and Caden is pretty much totally indifferent, now wearing the wig he caressed earlier, seemingly enjoying the ability he now has to drift into the shadows, anonymity, to observe the work and to assume a new identity. The notion of exploring little fractures in gender is not new for Kaufman, especially in *Being John Malkovich* and in lesser ways *Adaptation*. Caden's acknowledgment with Tammy earlier, that he thinks he might've been better at being a woman, that he'd like to be pretty the way Tammy's pretty, certainly paves the way for this shift; but there also seems to be a desire to let go of the work for Caden, as though the final step for him is handing the work off to his performers, his artists, these people he's assembled now around him. Though of course he doesn't wish to leave.

Minute 107

It's hard to say definitively whether what follows—a *somewhat* cliched though genuinely inspirational sermon from the priest overseeing the funeral, emphasizing interconnectedness and choice, and at one point gesturing directly at Caden when he advises figuring out his own divorce—is intended much in the way the Hollywood elements that slowly creep into *Adaptation* over its running time, that is, a bit, a critique of this tendency in art, toward final revelation, toward inspiration, toward leaving your audience feeling uplifted, inspired, and so on. It's possible, and probably even probable, but also kind of nice in the way of *Adaptation*, where we've endured Caden's suffering, or a representation of it anyway, much as he has, and now we're being allowed a bit of shaking up for our efforts. There's also this question of whether the work as it stood could've been realized. What's nice in this is it's not outside the realm of possibility that this *is* the work being realized, since it is, it's all a part of what Caden started however long ago. Millicent/Caden's address to Caden, too, and really this whole intervention into the work, supports a reading of *S.N.Y.* as coming from Millicent's perspective. I'd argue that there are elements of what the priest says that Caden might've liked to say, or do, in his life—a certain realizing of unconscious or repressed thinking. Because of the death-laden nature of the previous minutes it's undeniably *nice*, and comforting, I'd say, to have this shift in register. I think this, too, is a further benefit of working in such a capacious way, both for Caden and for Kaufman—and, by extension, for Aster and Tati and David Foster Wallace and countless others—since limitations on one's process might give firmer shape in the short term, but arguably revelatory moments like this, feelings like this of sitting with something and seeing it change and *open* and breathe, are simply not possible.

Minute 108

Our sermon continues, resolving—at least at the close of this minute—with Caden nodding quasi-emphatically at the priest's declaration: "Well, *fuck* everybody," and the supporting actors hum along as though they're at a church service. It does, I think, feel like a bit, but like Donald Kaufman's tragicomic "I got shot . . . isn't that fucked up?!" near the end of *Adaptation*, it's equal parts play and real emotive gesture. It's funny to see Caden, nodding along, sort of performing Millicent Weems/ Ellen Bascomb, in his wig. It's heavy and tragic too, to hear the sermonizing of the priest, the summation of a left spent in vague drift from thing to thing, waiting for whatever's supposed to be coming our way, surrounded by people who are too consumed with whatever's supposed to be coming their way to notice him, to open, and in turn to be that thing for someone else. We even see him sort of miming what's being performed, gesturing along with it like a mere fan of the work, truly receding into the role of an observer, and warming to this opportunity to not lord over the work any longer. It's interesting, too, since Millicent/Caden only briefly spoke with the priest, which means she couldn't possibly have given this entire monologue for his performing, which means that some of this is coming out of his having performed his role thus far, and his genuine identity, and his genuine perspective, which feels like another tick in favor of this being an actual realization of the work's potential, containing no longer only the things that Caden would say, but the vulnerable, earnest, spiritual expressions of these performers themselves. In Eco's initial use of musicians to segue into his fuller discussion of "the open work," there almost always seems to be this awkward moment of indecision on the part of performers of these pieces wherein they're assuming the confidence to take the thing and run with it. They're still performing, after all, a work by an artist in a recognized position of cultural authority to them. We see this even in performances online of John Cage's works, where they'll sometimes be playful—death metal bands performing "4'33"" with their massive amps plugged in and off, holding B. C. Rich Warlock guitars but playing nothing—or sometimes somber—most performances of his "Suite for Toy Piano" feel this way, even though it's written to be performed on a cheap children's instrument, which seems to call for play—but in every iteration there's a reverence implied since I can think of few better words to describe the lifework and output of Cage than "playful" and "sometimes somber." In the best cases of an "open work," though, such as Bernadette Mayer's *Utopia*, wherein she asked tons of friends to write whatever they wanted expressing their ideas for an ideal world, and assembled this with her own writing, democratically, alongside other discussions of Utopia by older thinkers, there are these multiple moments where coauthors, co-performers, assume a position of prominence, and begin to take over. Depending on how much we've grown to love our foibling Caden, it may irk us, but I don't think its discordance with the mood of the rest of the work is necessarily a bad thing.

Minute 109

The priest says "Amen," and all join in, and it begins to rain, and everyone takes out their black umbrellas, and then it cuts to Caden, seated with his assistant next to him, and Millicent/Caden, across from them. He tells them he's "out of ideas," that he's "dead," and this latter sounds more like a statement of fact than anything else. They sympathize with him, Millicent/Caden acknowledging that he's been doing very creative work for a very long time, that he's tired, that he just needs to rest for a bit, recalibrate, so that he might come back. As she's saying this, and the shift is clear, Caden's assistant moves to Millicent/Caden's side of the little table they're at, and pretty immediately the table in their conversation turns; Caden saying he'd like to keep his hand involved in the work somehow, and Millicent/Caden saying he could play Ellen, that they'd need someone to play her for at least a while. The assistant even says "It's a choice role!" attempting to convince this new aspirant that he should dive in, already really naturally and sweetly and funnily glomming onto Millicent/Caden since the whole thing is clearly shifted. In writing of this minute, I thought of course of the theory that exists about the film, that in some way it's happening in Millicent's consciousness, or that she's the one in control of the whole sprawl of it really. I then thought of the end of the film, which of course lines up with this line of thinking if you want it to, and more than anything I feel frustrated that I'd even looked into it, because though it might be interesting to consider—it isn't, really, to me, but others find it so and that's obviously not bad, necessarily—it's something that would only occur to someone who goes into a film attempting to solve it, to figure out its puzzle, instead of simply following it, and letting it happen to one, which seems a far better method for engaging art. There are two quotes from Tarkovsky that put this better than I probably can, so before the next minute I'll just offer those, and one more from Kubrick:

"Viewers search for meanings as if this was some sort of a charade. I know of no work of art whose meaning would be clear to the degree demanded by some. When they listen to music, read a novel or watch a play they frequently encounter fragments they don't understand. It's a normal state of the relationship toward a work of art. But when they go to the cinema—they demand complete clarity, total understanding. I am against discrimination in art. Clarity is not most important. The world created by an artist is as complex as the world that surrounds him.

People always try to find 'hidden' meanings in my films. But wouldn't it be strange to make a film while striving to hide one's thoughts? My images do not signify anything beyond what they are . . . We do not know ourselves that well: sometimes we express forces which cannot be grasped by any ordinary measure."

"If you look for a meaning, you'll miss everything that happens." (Andrei Tarkovsky)

"The feel of the experience is the important thing, not the ability to verbalize or analyze it." (Stanley Kubrick)

Minute 110

"I do like to clean," says Caden in response, and we get again a montage of his cleaning Adele's apartment. It's one of my favorite features of the third act of *S.N.Y.* that this is his return into their lives, an imaginary iteration of something he briefly did, once or perhaps twice, but now totally divorced from the reality of Adele and his home life, which doesn't exactly exist any longer, tragically. This is something I'll often do, that is, clean, when things are feeling strange for me, as though I'm unmoored from my home life, too much in my head in trying to figure out the problems of my writing, too far from the people in my life but not exactly ready to simply sit and face them and say something directly. I don't mean that I ignore the people in my life, my wife and my children. I don't ignore them. I'm conscious of my tendency to be sort of in my head about my work quite often, and with this consciousness I seem to have always insisted that I won't let myself become a cliched husband/father-writer, who picks one over the other and checks out from life on one side, or gives up on one side, because the primacy is obvious. In my case the primacy *is* obvious, but thankfully I don't drink and am not interested in gambling, or affairs, or other various excesses husband/father-artists have tended historically to get caught up in, and I think this has allowed me to manage. I'm medicated, which helps. Caden's medicated. But being aware of this potentiality, I am present, and I do try, and I'm mostly successful, and when I need to do something to get anchored again into my existence, it'll either be walking or cleaning something, tidying something up or doing something I've meant to do for a time. I do the dishes. I press down the garbage into the dumpster. I feed or clean the bunny cages. I let the dog out. Small things, I'm hardly cleaning the entire interior of an apartment, but there is something to this nevertheless. Caden sees the sweet old lady outside of the apartment, who might be the same sweet old lady from the real apartment, though it doesn't seem so, as she didn't seem sweet in that original context; she seemed Lynchian and menacing. Here she's sweet. She tells Caden to take this and to always keep it in, and he's unsure, and she gestures to put it in his ear, so he does, and he quickly understands it's a way for Millicent/Caden to speak to him. She tells him what to say to the woman, and he says it. It cuts then, and Caden is sitting on the toilet, and she tells him to "Reach for the toilet paper," and it of course makes one wonder whether she'd compelled him to go there and do those things. Outside of his window you can briefly see the warehouse, the roof—I'm not certain whether they're in warehouse 2 but I think they're in the main warehouse, but I guess technically if they're in one they're in the other, the warehouses I guess being a kind of synecdoche—and it's one of the most beautiful shots in the film; the ornate bathroom where Caden sits, the building facades just behind him, the large vaulted windows in the roof of the warehouse beyond, everything these rich granite grays, little hints of blue throughout, and you can see people in the window just across from Caden. It's wondrous.

Synecdoche, New York directed by Charlie Kaufman © Sony Pictures Classics 2008.

Minute 111

She continues speaking now, the warmth of her voice a clear comfort to Caden and certainly providing a comfort to any viewer. We see Caden as Ellen, and then we simply see Millicent, sitting in bed with a man we haven't seen thus far, presumably at home, having these conversations, speaking to Caden/Ellen, but simply out loud, in their home, as he sleeps in the bed next to her. She is talking about a wasted life, about what was supposed to happen, about having children, this kind of thing. We see her in the mirror. She asks the man, "Everything okay, Eric?" to which he replies, "Everything is everything," and she lets on her sense that she's disappointed him, that he hates her. Of course this supports reading the film as emanating from her perspective, and of course too it's not something I necessarily wish to fight anyone about, but my feeling is there's now such comfort in immersing himself in anyone other than himself, in Ellen, that it's overtaking him, and this thing that's so captivated him, that is, his life, his work, and that has always been my natural experience of *S.N.Y.*, which seems to me indicative that it's a nice thought, but not necessarily something that should overpower one's sense of the film, because devoting that much time to this, only to exit with a kind of "It was all a dream" blurry conclusion, or worse, that it was somehow a mental condition, seems insultingly reductive to a film that's anything but, that only seems to want to grow and to grow, outward, expanding. In Caden's, or in ours, or in the film's memory we now see the scene wherein Caden and Adele initially split up, and her statement that "Everyone is disappointing when you know someone," which is again certainly possible to read as something that burrowed itself down there and spun itself out narratively in Ellen's imagination to process her sense that she'd disappointed Eric in her present, but again feels like flushing a film that's too ambitious down the toilet once you've solved the puzzle, which often seems to be the impulse after such a reading. If a film is going to be capable of offering aphoristic truths about existence, as Kaufman's are, then there should need to be a slipperiness between voices, as there are in aphoristic literature, where we might not know who's speaking directly or about what as we sift through a work like *Bluets*, or even Gibran's *The Prophet*, but it doesn't matter so much as the devotion to its voice and that the weight of its statement is adequately conveyed.

Minute 112

I believe it's the most colorful moment in the film, when Millicent-as-herself-speaking-presumably-to-Caden reflects upon the memory of a picnic she had with her mother when she was young. Because one's eyes adjust to whatever visual palette we're presented, it isn't even totally apparent how much of the film is clouded over in grays, the bleak lights of the hospital basements bleeding out into the streets. There have been moments throughout, certainly, that brighten, but this one seems almost absurdly lush, like the opening sequence of *Blue Velvet*, with simple, bright yellows and reds highlighting the contrast. Millicent is feeling and accepting the regret of her life, that she did not have a child, and through this Caden is processing the loss of Olive, the two of their reflections moving back and forth, with finally Millicent weeping at the window as a kid moves by on the street below in soft focus. There's an aspect of the title that's sometimes mentioned as relevant here, that if the use of the word "synecdoche" is highly intentional, then maybe either Caden represents the whole, and Millicent represents the part, or conversely Millicent represents the whole, and Caden represents merely a part of her consciousness. I mention it because the term is so particular that people are bound to think about it, and the idea of characters themselves representing the concept seems sensible and has seemed sensible enough to me. I still tend to operate under the assumption that Caden is somehow a part representing the whole of what he's attempting to convey, that is the work, and through the work conveying an idealized version of his life. I no longer feel any real animus toward people striving to solve it, though, since engagement with it at all seems a positive thing, and this is the manner in which many people enjoy art. It's just the kind of thing that clouds my thinking, and nearing the end, with these sort of mournful-yet-optimistic tones *S.N.Y.* is now reaching, it seems to beckon for a nice clarity.

Minute 113

Most of this minute consists of Caden/Ellen lying in bed on the floor, presumably in the back closet of Adele's fake apartment, listening to Millicent/Caden's direction. She tells Caden/Ellen to look on the night table for a note from Adele, which is really a note informing Caden/Ellen that the night before Adele died of lung cancer. She tells him to reflect on the time she painted her/[your] portrait, how she'd made [you] feel beautiful for just a moment, and as Caden/Ellen rises from the mattress on the floor we begin to hear the noises of the ongoing conflict out on the street. He's been told that he can stay on, sort of because of Adele's death, it seems.

Minute 114

The apparent horror of the outside world has crept inside the work, the warehouses. Adele's fictive room is now overrun with rats. Caden leaves and makes a horrified sound as several of them burrow nearby, and the old woman, formerly so cheerful, stands there like a character in Lynch, saying in a drawling monotone, "There's nobody running the elevator anymore," and we see Caden begin the long walk down many flights of stairs. Everything has returned to its gray. Caden is not entirely bald on the top of his head. He'd seemingly fallen asleep sitting up between the last minute and this, as we heard noises of the conflict from the street, and when he wakes, his hair is changed. He looks up at the roof as he hears what sounds like people wanting to break through, revolutionaries shouting *Freedom!* slogans as the floors creak and sound as though they'll be inside in any moment. I'll say that the similar feeling I tend to have in response to rodents inside, in a best-case scenario, is followed by something similar to what Caden then undergoes. A kind of emotional bottoming out, an acceptance of one's state in the cosmos but also in the world, which is not ours, per se, not a thing we can expect always to be tailored to what we'd like it to be, which is perhaps slightly sad, but only just, and really is more healthy, a way of returning to a state of nature that can be warming if we let it.

Minute 115

"Everyone is everyone. So you are Adele, Hazel, Claire, Olive." Millicent narrates to Caden/Ellen as he walks from Adele's apartment, her voice entirely calm and accepting, a living embodiment of the kind of peace that only really seems to come with age. Caden's body is withering, his skin sagging, faltering, his hair thin, the most of the top of his head bald. The city in the warehouse is ruined. He sees a map to warehouse 2, on which is a small page, a tab he can lift to see that there's another warehouse, warehouse 3, somewhere in all of this. Again, I can imagine someone tempted to "solve" the thing because it's so elusive and yet particular, whereas, say, the abstraction of a film like *Tree of Life* feels like it calls less to us to solve its puzzle for its frequent sprawling feel. When something is abstract *and* particular, our inclination can be to treat it as a puzzle, a word game, a little problem we've got to solve; and yet in actually watching *Synecdoche, New York*, winding down now in this loving, human, mournful way, it seems such a reduction to try and do so. Cars are burned and burning in the street. Nobody's around. Everyone has left. And perhaps we are witnessing an elderly cleaning woman's final cleansing, her purging of this warped memory palace. I don't care. If we are *only* witnessing that, then I effectively stop caring, I don't wish to care. I am witnessing an artist who sort of failed and sort of did not fail in his great effort, his work, to open it and to liberate it into existence, his *Finnegans Wake*, his *The Owl in Daylight*, and everyone is everyone.

Minute 116

He continues walking, exploring this space. He finds a sheet of plastic enclosing a building with a rip in it and wanders through. The warehouse, the scale of it, its magnitude, is still a wonder to behold. This massive constructed thing, the beauty of his artwork, this thing to which there's been such devotion. And Millicent narrates over loss, her loss and Caden/Ellen's, the loss of people, the loss of loves, relationships. He finds a yellow golf cart, almost falling off a loading dock in the back of a building, and begins to drive, and for some reason I'm reminded of works like Renata Adler's *Speedboat*, where the fragmentation of consciousness is frequently tied to technology, and the presence of art—in Adler's case in the form of the prose novel, in Caden's in the form of a massive theater piece in a warehouse—is cut through by these strange human details, this intense observation of living in urban circumstance, trying and trying to find one's place within the world. The minute ends with a beautiful shot of the side of one of the buildings within the warehouse, Caden on the bottom in his yellow golf cart, driving across the frame.

Minute 117

Synecdoche, New York directed by Charlie Kaufman © Sony Pictures Classics 2008. All rights reserved.

Her speaking continues, as Caden/Ellen continues driving, looking throughout all the buildings, trying to find someone, anyone, as Millicent narrates: "Now you are here, it's 7:43 . . . Now you are here, it's 7:44" until finally Caden/Ellen sees someone, indistinct, standing in a sort of alley, quite large. There is certainly a sense of accepting the limitations of one's ambition, that is certain. There is a sense of having exhausted oneself, one's drive to create art, to create the work. "Where is everybody?" he asks her. "Mostly dead," she responds, and interestingly she almost looks like an amalgam of all the women we've seen in this film thus far, curly reddish-brown hair, a deeply empathetic face to Caden as he asks if she'll sit with him for a moment, that he's terribly lonely, terribly sad. Whatever is happening, it is depicting the death of this person we've watched and come to sometimes deeply admire, and certainly pity, and possibly even slightly detest. We've gone through so many disparate things with him, witnessed him trying in every dimension of his living, and now he sits, in a dismal place, with a seemingly kind woman, listening still to the direction, the narration telling him what to do.

Minute 118

"I feel like I know you . . ." he says to her. "Oh, uh, I was the, mother in uh, Ellen's dream . . ." [. . .] "There's everyone's dreams in all those apartments . . ." he says, staring off at the buildings on the horizon, thinking over this thing that's been constructed here, the work, this crazy ambitious project. "All those thoughts . . . I'll never know . . . That's the truth of it . . ." He looks and sees a clock drawn of chalk on a brick wall nearby, it's now 7:45—*Now you are here*. He tells her that he'd wanted to do that picnic with his daughter, though perhaps he's Ellen still, in his role. Now you are here.

Minute 119

He says that he feels he's disappointed her terribly. She's
generous, understanding, says "Oh no . . ." smiling,
understanding. "I love you," he says to her. She reciprocates.
Suddenly, as things begin to brighten slightly, to a lighter gray,
an almost white, he starts to say "I know how to do this play
now . . . I have an idea . . ." they begin fading further to the
white-gray, "I think . . . If everyone—" and Millicent interjects
as it shifts fully to its final light gray, saying only "Die." It closes,
holding on the light gray, as the credits begin to roll and the
song from throughout the film plays: "I'm just a little person . .
. One person, in a sea . . ." and a simple piano plays. Whatever it
is, whatever it *means*, can and must only be in one's subjective
relationship to it—that's all there is, that's all we finally have.
We hold, we listen, respecting the many individuals who've
worked on this film—it isn't only Kaufman, it's hundreds of
people, and Philip Seymour Hoffman, now gone, and likely the
greatest actor of his generation, and delivering one of if not his
greatest performance ever—we listen, warming, listening. We
think of all that Caden did, that all of them did, and tried to
do. And finally we do think of Charlie Kaufman, in pursuit of
something to contain all the world, all of the vexing subjectivity

of being a person, of having a body, of being an artist, a dad, a husband, of trying to navigate these things and to make sense of them. We consider him, and in our way we do love him—we close our eyes.

> *Whoever has no house now, will never have one.*
> *Whoever is alone will stay alone,*
> *will sit, read, write long letters through the evening,*
> *and wander the boulevards, up and down,*
> *restlessly, while the dry leaves are blowing.*

NOTES

Minutes 1–119

1 Kaufman, C. & Jonze, S. (Producer), & Kaufman, C. (Director) (2008). *Synecdoche, New York*. United States: Sony Pictures Classics.

2 Rilke, Rainer Maria (2013). "Autumn Day." *The Selected Poetry of Rainer Maria Rilke*. London: Vintage.

3 Lahr, John (1999). "Arthur Miller and the Making of Willy Loman." *The New Yorker*, January 17.

4 Guillen, Michael (2008). "Synecdoche, New York—Interview with Charlie Kaufman." *TwitchFilm.net*, October 23. Archived from the original on September 7, 2010.

5 Williams, Tennessee (1964). *The Milk Train Doesn't Stop Here Anymore*. New York: Dramatists Play Service Inc.

6 Grotowski, J. (2002). *Towards a Poor Theatre* (1st ed.). London: Routledge.

7 Samuel Beckett (1988). *Krapp's Last Tape*. New York: Pennebaker Associates.

8 Artaud, Antonin (2013). *The Theatre and Its Double*. Richmond, England: Alma Classics.

9 Sylvia Plath, "Ariel" from *Collected Poems*. Copyright © 1960, 1965, 1971, 1981 by the Estate of Sylvia Plath. Editorial matter copyright © 1981 by Ted Hughes. Used by permission of HarperCollins Publishers.

10 Eco, Umberto (1989). *The Open Work*. Cambridge, MA: Harvard University Press.

11 LeBlanc, Larry (2018). "In the Hot Seat with Larry LeBlanc: Brian Eno, musician, artist, producer, thinker." *Celebrity Access*, July 19. https://celebrityaccess.com/2018/07/19/brian-eno/.

INDEX

136

INDEX